Sew A Beautiful Wedding

by Gail Brown and Karen Dillon

designed by Linda Wisner

illustrated by Lin Brink
Kathy Kifer Howell
Linda Wisner

D1041024

With love to our husbands and biggest fans, Steve Simpson and Tony Dillon

Special thanks to Bobbie Keeney, our reliable typist, and to Blue Ridge Winkler, Butterick Fashion Marketing Company (Butterick and Vogue patterns), Embassy Trimmings, Hoffman Fabrics, Emil Katz & Co., Mandel Fabrics, Martin Velvets, McCall Patterns Company, Rosewood Fabrics, Simplicity Pattern Company, Inc., Springs Mills Inc. Retail and Specialty Fabrics Division, Thompson of California, and William E. Wright Company.

The brand names of products mentioned in this book are those we've personally tested and liked. We are, however, not subsidized by any company. There may be other products that are comparable, even better sewing aids or that may be developed after the printing of this book.

The fashion illustrations in this book are not intended to represent commercial patterns, although similar styles very possibly may be available.

*Gail
Brown*

*Karen
Horton
Dillon*

About the Authors

Home economists Gail Brown and Karen Horton Dillon are nationally known sewing experts who have considerable experience sewing for weddings. They have consulted on and sewn for innumerable weddings, including their own.

While working toward her Clothing and Textile Degree at the University of Washington, Gail worked in the alterations and custom dressmaking department of a bridal specialty shop. After graduation, a move to New York landed her a job as the promotional consultant, then Marketing Director, for Stretch & Sew, Inc., wrote another Palmer/Pletsch book, "Sensational Silk," co-authored "The Super Sweater Idea Book" for Butterick Publishing and "Instant Interiors" a home decorating how-to series. Now she is a partner of Brown/Wisner, an Oregon-based creative service agency specializing in sewing-related projects, and frequently appears on both cable and network television.

Karen has been in the fashion/sewing field since her graduation from Montana State University — first in retail sales with large department stores then in education with The Armo Co., a New York shaping fabrics manufacturer. For several years she was the Sewing Consultant for New York Fabrics near San Francisco, where, through her consumer programs, she gained a wide reputation among Bay Area home sewers for her expertise on bridal fabrics and sewing. She now travels throughout North America for Palmer/Pletsch Associates teaching sewing and decorating seminars. She is affiliated with Fashion Group, American Home Economics Association and Home Economists in Business.

— Both were "homesewn" brides and are happily married!

Table of Contents

Yes, You Can Sew A Beautiful Wedding

Though some say marriage and weddings are going out of style, figures show otherwise — marrying and remarrying are dramatically on the increase. Ideas concerning traditional and not-so-traditional wedding rituals are changing constantly, but it seems that the ceremony and the institution are more popular than ever.

For each of the millions of weddings annually there is a bride and groom who had fantasies about how their wedding would look and be . . . foremost of course, the wedding attire which set the "tone" for the whole ceremony.

But for most, wedding dreams have had to be compromised. . . particularly in regard to the bride's gown and her attendants' attire. Ready-to-wear dresses can be prohibitively expensive and are available in limited style and size ranges. And if time is a factor, as it is for many weddings, special ordering and alterations can be risky at best.

We wrote this book so that every couple could have the beautiful wedding they've dreamed of, affordably, just as we were able to do. Cost savings for home sewing in relation to ready-to-wear gowns can range up to 80% — not to mention the extra advantages of limitless design choices and custom fitting for the entire wedding party.

A Cost Comparison

We selected similar gowns for our cost comparison — although cost differences will differ with style and fabric choices, you can count on considerable savings for both the bride's and bridesmaids' dresses.

Save up to 80% when sewing your own gown.

Custom-made*   # Ready-to-wear

Gown

Lace (French re-embroidered)
1⅞ yds. @$39.00/yd for
  bodice (36″ wide) $73.00
2¼ yds. @$11.00/yd.
  for hem 24.00

Fabric (Peau de Soie)
5½ yds. @$4.50/yd.
(45″ wide)............................ 24.75

Trimmings (Pearls)
4 packages @ .50 ....2.00

Notions
Zipper, hooks/eyes,
buttons (11), shoulder
pads, thread, needles,
horsehair 7.00

Pattern 7.50

      Gown SUB TOTAL $138.25

(Alterations on
ready-to-wear can
be expensive —
include when
calculating costs.)

The gown $700.00

Slip

3½ yds. 100% polyester
lining @ 2.70/yd. $9.45

Slip
(separate) $25.00

Headpiece/Veil

Fabric/trim —
Scraps from dress $0.00
Plain Buckram Frame 2.00
Tulle — 5 yds. @ 2.00/yd.
(108″ wide).............................10.00

  Headpiece/Veil
  SUB TOTAL $12.00

Headpiece/Veil $80.00

Custom-made
TOTAL....................... $159.70

Ready-to-wear
TOTAL $805.00

Cost Difference........ ..645.30
A Saving of...................... 81%

*A dressmaker's fee would add to the total cost of the gown (Estimates given for a size 10)

Sure It Costs Less, But Isn't Sewing For A Wedding Difficult?

No. Sewing a wedding gown and the bridesmaids' dresses can be easy.

There was a time when sewing for a wedding meant hours and hours of tedious handwork to re-embroider laces, sew pin tucks and crochet tiny buttons.

Now, with the techniques borrowed from manufacturers and the latest sewing advances — all presented in this book — anyone can create a beautiful wedding, from the bridal gown to the mother of the bride's dress.

Some traditional gowns may require more sewing time (although our bridal sewing shortcuts will show you how easy pearls, lace, and gathers can be) but more informal wedding fashions can be "made" in hours. In fact, many bridal fabrics and gowns should be handled as little as possible, so you'll press, interface and underline less!!

Whatever your choice, you'll be confident that your custom-made gown and the entire wedding party attire, are original, look great, fit better and cost less than their ready-to-wear alternatives.

Have a beautiful wedding!

Gail Brown and Karen Dillon

I. Bridal Planning Checklist
featuring Your Sewing Timeline

Perhaps the most important key to an enjoyable, beautiful and relaxed (?) wedding is planning. We cannot stress enough how important it is to start planning as soon as you set your wedding date. Certainly many weddings today do not and cannot involve months and months of planning, particularly in light of the decrease in formal engagements. Still, even the smallest wedding necessitates preparation. Of course, the larger the wedding the more urgent planning becomes.

When Karen announced her engagement, she had five months to plan. But she remembers helping a bride who had one week to plan a wedding and sew a gown. She did it! She even finished a going-away outfit. Gail had only one month to prepare and was amazed how much planning her tiny at-home ceremony required.

To make your planning easier, we have compiled a list of "things to do" and "when" for everything — from buying your gown fabric to scheduling a photographer. Some of the items obviously do not involve sewing, but since all planning is interrelated, we decided to develop one really comprehensive plan that would cover all areas. But remember, this checklist is only designed to be a guideline to make your job easier. Times are changing and there are no longer hard and fast rules for brides and weddings.

4-6 MONTHS BEFORE

The Wedding, Location and Date

- After engagement, target wedding date.

- Decide with your fiancé the size, style and budget of the wedding you want. Also discuss the budget details with whomever will be paying the bills, if other than yourselves. Make a list of anticipated expenses.

- Select attendants from among your closest friends and/or relatives. Generally one usher is needed for every 50 guests. There need not be the same number of bridesmaids as ushers.

- Photocopy the names, addresses and phone numbers of all attendants and distribute them to friends and relatives for ready references — you'll want them included in many pre-wedding activities.

- Make arrangements with your minister, rabbi or judge for wedding date (have alternative dates in mind).

- Contact church, hall, hotel, restaurant or club regarding wedding, rehearsal and reception dates. Most schedule months in advance. Records show that for larger weddings, on the average ¼ of the guests invited will not attend (this can effect your location choice). If an at-home wedding, plan for decor changes and cleaning for both indoors and outdoors.

- Once date is scheduled at location, double-check decorating and refreshment restrictions, if any.

- Plan color scheme for wedding and reception (Chapter V).

- Decide on and schedule music for wedding and reception.

- Arrange and confirm date with a photographer for your engagement photo, bridal portrait, wedding pictures, etc.

- Contact newspaper society editor about your engagement and forthcoming wedding. Ask if they accept engagement photos.

- Interview prospective florist and service caterer. Discuss price, service expectations, dates. Ask these establishments for list of referrals. Get all financial statements in writing.

Your Gown, Wedding Party Attire

- Start trying on ready-made dresses to determine the most flattering style and color.

- Look in pattern books for a style(s) similar to those you've seen and liked in bridal departments and magazines.

- Study what colors are available for ushers and coordinate to bridesmaids' attire.

- Make an appointment with the bridal consultant in a favorite fabric store during "quiet hours" so she can devote time to your needs. You may want to have your maid of honor and/or your mother accompany you (also, your dressmaker, if you aren't the seamstress).

- Discuss pattern and fabric possibilities with the consultant and ask for swatches for future referral. Attach swatches to pages 125-127.

- After studying the fabrics and patterns, make final choices for your gown and the wedding party. Discuss garments and price ranges if your attendants are buying their own dresses.

- Buy or special order fabric — remember, special orders can take several weeks.

- Provide mothers of the bride and groom with color swatches, formality guidelines and style selections so that they might harmonize outfits.

The Honeymoon

Make your honeymoon travel plans early.

- Talk to a travel agent about your honeymoon plans. Most bargain fares and bookings are available only if you reserve and pay months in advance.

- Plan and buy fabrics for your honeymoon wardrobe.

Rings

- Select rings with your fiance.

Guest List, Announcements, Invitations, Thank-Yous

- Decide on type of announcements, invitations, etc. after talking with a printer (we recommend taking care of all your printing needs at this time, i.e. invitations and envelopes, reception enclosures, thank you notes, at-home cards, etc.). No longer are engraved invitations considered de rigueur; there are other more affordable, creative styles available (ask for offset or ITEK printing).

- Begin making up your wedding list so that invitations can be addressed just as soon as they are printed (each should be handwritten). Don't underestimate the amount of time you'll need for addressing (ask groom and/or attendants to help).

- Register for wedding gifts at department and gift stores.

2-4 MONTHS BEFORE

The Wedding, Location and Date

- Give fiancé his "Things-to-do" list (i.e., men's wedding attire).

- Plan for rehearsal dinner/party (the week of the wedding). This can be informal and serve as a special "thank you" for helpers and out-of-town guests.

- Marriage license, honeymoon arrangements, new apartment or home, etc.

Pin fit your gown.

Your Gown, Wedding Party Attire

- Make arrangements to have one person cut out and sew all the attendants' attire — you can save on yardage and all the dresses will look alike.

- Pre-shrink fabric, if necessary.

- Buy your wedding shoes and lingerie.

- Lay out, cut out and pin fit your gown, wearing your wedding lingerie and shoes. Begin sewing.

- Supervise the fittings of the bridesmaids' dresses.

The Honeymoon

- Start sewing your "going-away" and honeymoon clothes.

Guest List, Announcements, Thank-Yous

- Check to see that your invitations, thank-yous, etc., have arrived . . . keep up that addressing.

- Arrange lodging for out-of-town relatives and guests.

1 MONTH BEFORE

The Wedding, Location and Date

- Get marriage license and blood tests.

- Reconfirm all arrangements with florist, caterer, location, clergyman and photographer.

- If necessary, make name and address changes for all mail, checking accounts, subscriptions, etc.

- Contact society/women's editor about your wedding announcement. Most newspapers want them at least 10 days before the wedding. Be sure to include a release date. Request their standard form if available.

- Have bridal portrait taken.

Apply beads with glue

Your Gown, Wedding Party Attire

- Apply finishing touches to your gown and headpiece. Check for "walkability" of wedding shoes, fit and color blend of lingerie.

- Make sure all ushers have been fitted for their suits, and attendants' attire is completed.

The Honeymoon

- Complete wardrobe for "going-away" and honeymoon.

Guest List, Announcements and Thank-Yous

- Mail all wedding, reception invitations.

- Start sending out thank-you notes to party hostesses and for incoming gifts.

- Buy/make gifts for your fiancé, bridesmaids, ushers.

- Take pictures of your wedding preparations — you'll enjoy looking back on these year after year.

1 WEEK BEFORE

The Wedding, Location and Date

- Save this week for parties, visits from friends, family.

Your Gown, Wedding Party Attire

- Your dress is done and looks beautiful — last minute wedding worries should not include an unfinished gown.

- Treat yourself to some personal luxuries — facial, manicure, hair done. We do not suggest, however, changing your style dramatically for the wedding . . . look natural!

- Gather all the things you will need for your wedding day — a pressed, clean gown, make-up, lingerie, safety pins, needle & thread, hair pins, shoes, extra hose (all your attendants should do the same).

- Have fun at the rehearsal dinner/party. Leave your marriage license with the clergyman.

The Honeymoon

- Get your going-away clothes, luggage, handbag, etc. packed and ready while you are still thinking clearly. Confirm travel reservations.

Guest List, Announcements, Thank-Yous

- Don't forget to give personal thanks to all those who are and will be helping you.

THE WEDDING DAY

- If you haven't already, bring your marriage license!

- All the details have been covered . . . enjoy the excitement of your big day.

YOU'RE MARRIED

Capture wedding memories in photographs

- As soon as you select your wedding photo, send it, and the ceremony information to the paper.

- All thank-you notes should be sent within two months of your wedding date.

- Protect your gown by having it cleaned and properly stored.

II. Your Wedding Image

Your Wedding Image:
The Gown Type

After determining with your groom and family the type of wedding you'll have . . . start thinking about your gown. The gown style you choose should relate to the degree of formality of your wedding — a trainless, "garden/country look" worn without a headpiece would not be appropriate for a formal evening wedding. But any of the gown types can be made more or less formal depending on fabric choice and accessories.

We've categorized bridal gowns into the four most distinct types. Select from our gown types the "image" you desire, then refer to the Figure Flattering Style Recommendations (pages 21-29) to coordinate the best possible bridal look for you.

It is easy to change the mood of a garment style by selecting a different fabric. A simple gown with fitted bodice and gathered skirt made in satin has a romantic image, while the same design made in eyelet has a country look. The mood and image you wish to present depends then, on both your fabric type and color, plus the style choice(which may be the combination of several patterns).To select the right combination,use the guidelines that follow featuring "wedding gown types" and "suggested fabrics and trims".

Marrying Again

As we've said before, there are no more hard and fast rules of etiquette for brides. In days past, it was said that second-time brides should not wear formal white gowns and veils, invite hundreds of people or toss a bouquet. But times, attitudes and brides have changed.

Your choice of a wedding gown is up to you, your fiance' and your families. Many second-time brides wanting a "toned down" ceremony, wear a colored contemporary gown, a simple headpiece or none at all, have one attendant and fewer guests. Others look forward to a very traditional ceremony and gown, possibly having missed the opportunity the first time.

WEDNG GOWN TYPES

CLASSIC/ TRADITIONAL
can be formal or semi-formal

Clean, simple lines; re-embroidered lace and beading through the bodice and sleeve areas; generally long-sleeved; chapel, cathedral or sweep length trains and veils.

Suggested Fabrics

Brocade
Crepe
Faille
Ottoman
Peau de soie
Satin
Sheers — soft & crisp
Silks — shantung, worsted
Taffeta
Re-embroidered laces

Trims

Beading
Fur
Lace appliqués and edging

ROMANTIC
can be formal or semi-formal

"Picture book" styling typified by full, swirling skirts adorned with ruffles and ribbons; fitted bodice with elaborate sleeve detail; shaped neckline; puffed sleeves; soft veils, picture hats and parasols.

Suggested Fabrics

"Antique" lace
Brocade
Crepe
Crocheted laces
Domestic "all-over"
    lace yardage
Imported laces
Peau de soie
Qiana®
Satin — light and
    medium weight
Sheers — soft, crisp
Silks
Taffeta
Moire'

Trims

Feathers
Pleated
Ruffled flounces
Lace appliqués
    and edging

18

UPDATED/ CONTEMPORARY

can be semi-formal or informal

Soft, refined fabric textures in late afternoon or evening clothes styling; straight silhouettes; may be short dress or jacketed; generally little or no lace; can be very dramatic, i.e., one flower bouquet or a close-fitting headpiece with no veil.

Suggested Fabrics

Challis
Crepe
Knits
Pleated fabrics
Polyester silkies
Silk — crepe de chine, charmeuse
Sheers — soft or filmy

Trims

Crocheted lace
Feathers
Fur
Metallic, beaded accents

GARDEN/
COUNTRY LOOK
can be semi-formal or informal

Simplified styling in crisp fabrics, dainty tucks and trim detail; fitted bodices; sleeveless to long sleeved; may not have a train or veil; head-piece can be simply a flower wreath.

Suggested Fabrics

Batiste
Broadcloth
Cotton laces
Embroidered fabrics
English net
Eyelet laces
Gauze
Gingham
Lace curtains or tablecloths
Lawn
Linen
Muslin
Polished cotton

Trims

Crocheted laces
Eyelet trim
Beading lace
Ribbons

III. Choosing the Most Flattering Style
for You and Your Attendants

We all come in different shapes and sizes . . . a "perfect" size 10 is hard to find.

Choosing the most flattering style(s) for you and your attendants is one of the most important planning decisions you will make. Not only will it effect how comfortable and attractive you all will feel, but it will also be the most influential factor in your photos — the only visual memory of your wedding day. To make your job easier, we've given style recommendations for specific heights and proportions. . .certain design lines and fabrics enhance each figure type.

REMEMBER, your bridesmaids' dresses should have the same feeling as your gown but don't have to be an exact copy. Think in terms of the gown types on pages 17-20. A slender bride has much more design flexibility than over-weight attendants. Keep their figure types in mind. More often than not they're paying for the dresses and want to look their very best — on the wedding day and possibly for other occasions. Don't forget to take a long, hard look at your own figure too! Identify not only your general body type, but particular figure problems, i.e., large bustline, sloping shoulders, etc.

Study the recommendations we've given for different figure types, then select the silhouette, neckline, sleeve, train and back interest for your gown and the attendants. Your bridesmaids should have supplied you with their measurements and heights (see notebook section for handy reference).

Figure-Flattering Style Recommendations
SLENDER/SHORT

LOOK FOR simple design lines and fabrics that give the illusion of height.

- Silhouettes with vertical lines that add height; A-line, princess, straight-line.

- Consider designs that draw the eye upward — bodice or neckline detail with lace, beading or trim.

- Pin tucked front bodice panels create the illusion of height.

- Fingertip or longer veil; trim edge to create a vertical line.

- Fitted sleeves — long fitted, capped, trumpet, leg-o-mutton.
- A high headpiece adds height. (It shouldn't be overly full however.)
- Vertical necklines -"V", keyhole, wrap, scoop.
- Choose soft, fluid fabrics — knits, sheers, gauze, supple brocades, soft lace, crepe.
- Wear delicate higher-heeled shoes.
- Cathedral-length train or shorter won't overwhelm.

AVOID design lines and fabrics that make the figure appear shorter and wider:

- "Too-full" sleeves.
- Gathered tiered skirt, deep hem ruffle.
- Wide cumberbunds.
- Heavy lace fabric or trim that overpowers your size.
- Big flowers and large bouquets.
- Very crisp, stiff fabrics.
- Large scale prints.
- Heavily textured fabrics — linen, heavy laces, damask, velvet, etc.

FULL-FIGURED/ SHORT

LOOK FOR design lines and fabrics that make the figure look longer and leaner.

- Silhouette lines that are vertical — A-line, princess, straight-line are best.
- Fit should skim the body, never be too tight. (A well-fitting bra will help!)
- Slender sleeves — long, fitted.
- "V", scoop, keyhole, wrap neckline.
- A fabric with a dull finish that's fluid — crepe, knits, some soft sheers.
- High headpiece with fingertip or longer veil. Do not trim veil edge.
- Bouquet of small-medium size.

AVOID design lines that draw the eye horizontally across the figure or fabrics that are bulky or clingy.

- Bouffant silhouettes.
- Large scale prints.
- Heavily textured fabrics—velvets, quilted looks, heavy laces.
- Shiny fabrics.
- Lace trims at hemline, tiers, ruffles.
- Tiered skirts.
- Ruffled necklines.
- Cathedral or sweeptrains.
- Very full veils.

AVERAGE/AVERAGE

Most styles will fit and flatter you. . .concentrate on particular figure problems when choosing styles.

FULL-FIGURED/ AVERAGE

LOOK FOR continuous vertical design lines and smooth, fluid fabrics that "minimize" the figure.

- Silhouettes that direct attention to the face—princess, A-line and straight-line.
- Dresses should fall smoothly and gently over the hips—not tight.
- "V", scoop, keyhole (with or without Queen Anne collar), wrap necklines.
- Headpiece should provide height to balance body size.
- Soft fluid fabrics are good—knits with body, crepes, sheers, antique satin (dull finish).
- Any length train—but it shouldn't be excessively full.

AVOID design lines that chop the figure up horizontally, or "fattening" fabrics that add weight.

- Too huge or very tiny design.

- Ruffles around neckline, sleeve or skirt which add bulk and create horizontal lines.

- A "baby doll" look.

- Bulky fabric which adds weight; heavy laces, fur, crocheted looks, velvets/velveteen.

- Very shiny fabrics—satins, taffetas, brocades.

SLENDER/TALL

You have a model's figure, so most styles are flattering. However, you may want to appear shorter in relation to your groom.

LOOK FOR design lines that run around the body and textured fabrics that make the figure appear "fuller".

- Bouffant or full princess or A-line silhouettes.

- If you prefer a controlled silhouette, make it an A-line with trim and appliqué going around the body.

- Ruffled, gathered tiers or peplum — any horizontal line detail will minimize height.

- Any length train—although you are able to wear the fullest sweep type.

- Select full, long or three-quarter length sleeves—can fill in a too-slender body.

- Heavy, re-embroidered laces, peau de soies, velvets, satins.

- Blouson variation of the straight-line silhouette.

- Sashed or belted waistlines.

- Deep ruffle trims.

- Increase length and fullness of veil — a fuller, longer one may shorten your appearance.

- Wear your gown with bustle back slip.

AVOID design lines and fabrics that will overemphasize your height and thinness.

- Severe angular lines—a straight-line silhouette can be flattering if the lines are soft, i.e., a blouson.

- Very tailored looks.

24

- A blusher length veil can look too short.

FULL-FIGURED/TALL

LOOK FOR design lines and fabrics that make the figure look more slender.

- A-line, straight-line, or princess line silhouettes.
- "V", scoop, keyhole necklines can be flattering.
- Soft knits, crepe, peau de soie, silk worsted, etc.

AVOID designs "out-of-scale" with your size or fabrics that add weight to the figure.

- Short puffed, leg-o-mutton or very full bishop sleeves.
- Cinched waists and cumberbunds.
- Clingy jersey fabrics.
- "Baby doll" look, can look out of place on a large woman.
- Very shiny or bulky fabrics, heavy laces.

QUEEN SIZE

(heavier than full figured, size 18+ or if you think you could lose 25+ pounds)

LOOK FOR clean, simple design lines that "play down" your size and figure—choose fabrics that just skim the body contours. Bring the focus to your face!

- Princess line, A-line or straight-line silhouettes.
- Straight or fitted sleeves (not too tight).
- A trim fit—not too tight or too loose.
- Any length train.
- Fine lace can be used for neckline, bodice and hem trim.

- Off-white or pastel—bright white reflects the most light making the figure appear larger.

- Lower necklines—scoop, camisole, keyhole, "V", wrap.

- A simple veil with not too much fullness (mantillas can be lovely).

- The "layered look" done with layers of lightweight fabrics.

- For attendants, darker colors can minimize the body size.

> NOTE: Adapt large or women's size dress patterns for bride's or bridesmaids' gowns.

AVOID busy design lines that add weight to the figure and bulky fabrics.

- "Little girl" or "baby doll" looks.

- A "too-tight" fit.

- Very clingy fabrics.

- Ruffles and trims encircling the body.

- Gathered skirts.

- Fabrics with dramatic texture or sheen like satins, taffetas, plush velvets, heavy laces.

- Very high, tight fitting necklines like Gibson, mandarin, cowl, etc.

- A very full train.

> NOTE: For any queen size person, we recommend *Sew Big* by Marilyn Thelen (order information on last page).

Particular Figure Problems

SLOPING SHOULDERS

LOOK FOR shoulder/bodice detail that make the shoulders look more square.

- Establish width at the shoulder/neckline with a headpiece/hairdo that is full.

- Horizontal design lines through the shoulder/neckline area—yokes, square necklines, circular or square yokes, camisoles, etc.

- Extended shoulder lines—cap sleeves, yokes, ruffles, capelets.

- Set-in sleeves with gathered sleeve caps can widen the shoulder area—leg-o-mutton, Gibson, baby doll, etc.

- Trim natural waistline — silhouette definition that will make the shoulders look broader, proportionately.
- Soft shoulder pads.

AVOID styles that over-expose or emphasize the slope of your shoulders.

- Sleeveless, halter or strapless style gowns (it can be difficult to balance the width of your skirt with no sleeves).
- Raglan sleeves.
- High necklines can (not always) bring attention to sloping shoulders.

NOTE: Stand up straight, shoulders back!

BUSTY

LOOK FOR styles that trim the bustline making it look smaller and in balance with the rest of your figure.

- A smooth fit (but not tight) through the bodice area.
- "V", scoop, keyhole, wrap necklines.
- A properly fitted, minimizing bra.
- Fitted sleeves (full sleeves can make you look bustier).
- Fabrics like soft fluid knits, crepes, peau de soie, organdy, gauze, etc.
- Tailored styles can look elegant on a busty figure.
- Sloping waistline.

AVOID styles and fabrics that add weight or draw more attention to the bust.

- Napped, ultra-shiny fabrics or heavy lace for the bodice.
- Cinched natural waistlines (in proportion, can make the bust look larger)
- Empire lines that are fitted under the bust.
- Clingy jersey.
- Sheer fabrics that reveal bra lines.
- Any superfluous detail at the neckline or bustline—jewelry, ruffles, pleats, shirring.
- Puffed, Victorian or Gibson sleeves.
- Revealing necklines.

SMALL BUSTLINE

LOOK FOR styles and fabrics that will add "visual dimension" to the bustline.

- Medium to heavy laces for the bodice/sleeve areas.

- Gathers, pleats and ruffles that fill in the bustline.

- Set-in full sleeves help define bodice width.

- A defined natural waistline can make the bust, in contrast, look larger (avoid if your waist is large).

- Square, camisole, yoked, high necklines can make the bust look larger.

- Full or elaborate veils and headpieces.

- Consider wearing a bra that adds a little.

- Full sleeves—leg-o-mutton, puffed, Victorian and Gibson can add fullness to the bodice area.

AVOID styles that make your bust look flat and small (especially if the rest of your body isn't).

- Filmy, soft fabrics through the bustline area.

- Tight fitting bodices without detail.

- Overly tailored bodices.

- Very full skirt—could make the bustline look too small proportionately unless balanced by bodice width (shoulder ruffles, yokes, etc.).

- Low-cut scoop and "V" necklines.

TUMMY/HEAVY MIDRIFF

LOOK FOR design lines that focus the eye away from the tummy area.

- Princess line silhouettes.

- Skirt fullness that camouflages tummy/midriff.

- Sloping waistline (raised in the front to lower in the back).

- Figure control undergarment and gown lining.

- Neckline and headpiece detail.
- Fabrics that have body but aren't bulky—heavy crepes, knits, lightweight laces, antique satin, peau de soie.
- Full bouquet can hide tummy (great for photographs).

AVOID styles that reveal or highlight the tummy area.

- Natural waistline style gowns.
- Straight-line silhouette gowns can reveal heavy midriff.
- Any garment that fits too closely to the tummy/midriff area.
- Blouson bodices.
- Wide midriff cumberbunds.
- Full or bell sleeves can draw attention to the waist/tummy area.

SHORT NECK

LOOK FOR styles that will make your neck appear longer.

- Scoop, wrap, "V", or keyhole necklines that visually elongate the neck.
- If hair is long, it should be up and away from the face.
- A higher headpiece can create the illusion of a longer neck.

AVOID styles that cover up the neck, making it appear even shorter.

- High or jewel necklines or stand-up collars like Victorian.
- Wearing choker necklace or ribbon tie.
- Hairstyles that cover up the neck.

IV. Sketch the Gown

A Few Important Reminders

Most of the brides we've helped must combine patterns to get all the style features they want. Here's an easy way to do it:

Remember paper dolls? Our technique is much the same. Take a piece of tissue paper and transfer the "Traceable Bride" (or bridesmaid) silhouette of your choice. Trace the neckline, sleeve, waist, train and back interest features. After tracing the gown (this might take a few tries and sheets of tracing paper), then sketch in the headpiece (pages 113-114) and veil. In Chapter VI, we will explain how to combine the patterns you have purchased that have these different style features.

• Your back should be beautiful. Most brides don't realize that the entire wedding party will be seen more from the back than the front. That's why trains, bows, laces and veils adorn the back of most ready-to-wear gowns. Some patterns don't have back interest (especially if you've chosen styles not designated for bridal wear). You may want to add some, or wear a more decorative headpiece or hairdo. Very long hair can cover up the style features of a gown and can detract from the consistent look of your party. Consider wearing hair up and suggesting it to your attendants.

• Most apparent to your guests will be poor-fitting clothes, the wrong under-garments, wrinkles, unsightly hem stitches — all great reasons to sew your own!

• Keep referring to the Figure Flattery Recommendations while choosing the gown style features.

The Traceable Bride
(or bridesmaid)

Trace this figure and your
desired silhouette.

Princess line inner seaming
Straight-line
A-line
Princess
Bouffant

Trace the
back of
your desired
silhouette.

Princess line inner seaming

Straight-line

A-line

Princess

Bouffant

Traceable Waistlines

By far the most flattering waistline on most brides is the "sloping" style — that's why you'll see it so frequently in ready-made designs.

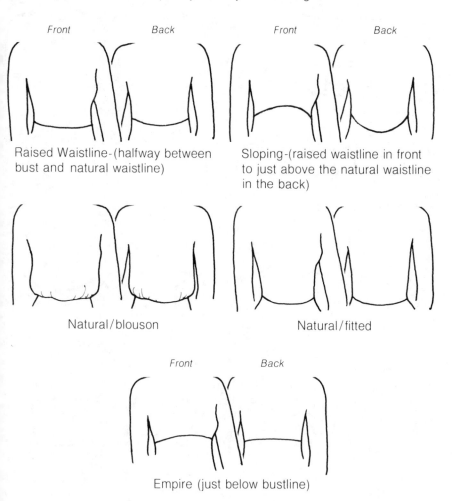

Raised Waistline - (halfway between bust and natural waistline)

Sloping - (raised waistline in front to just above the natural waistline in the back)

Natural / blouson

Natural / fitted

Empire (just below bustline)

Traceable Necklines

Beware of necklines that are too revealing. The clergyman stands above you and it could be too distracting.

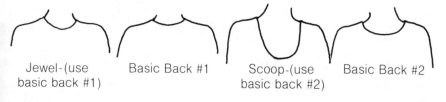

Jewel - (use basic back #1)

Basic Back #1

Scoop - (use basic back #2)

Basic Back #2

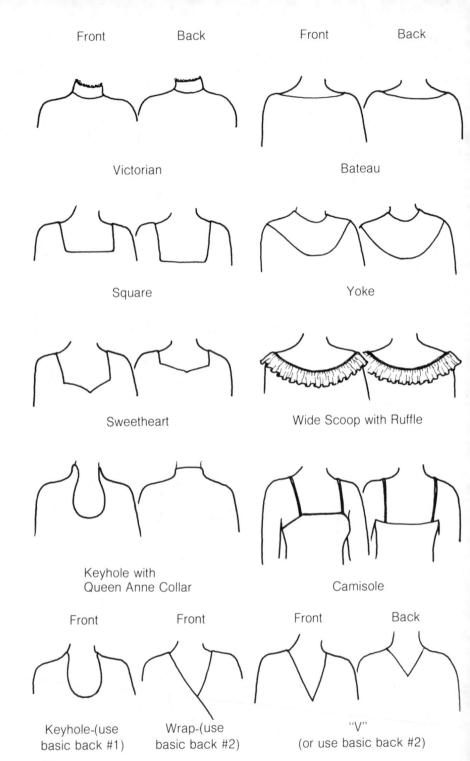

Front   Back   Front   Back

Victorian   Bateau

Square   Yoke

Sweetheart   Wide Scoop with Ruffle

Keyhole with
Queen Anne Collar   Camisole

Front   Front   Front   Back

Keyhole-(use
basic back #1)   Wrap-(use
basic back #2)   "V"
(or use basic back #2)

34

Traceable Sleeves

When sketching your gown(s), the back of the sleeve is essentially the same as the front.

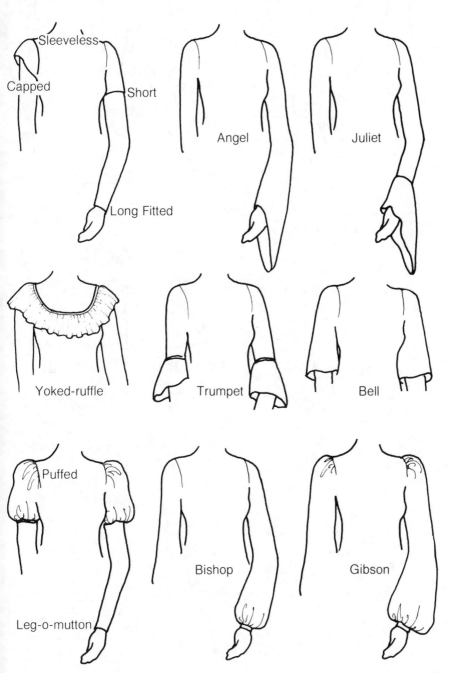

Sleeveless

Capped

Short

Angel

Juliet

Long Fitted

Yoked-ruffle

Trumpet

Bell

Puffed

Bishop

Gibson

Leg-o-mutton

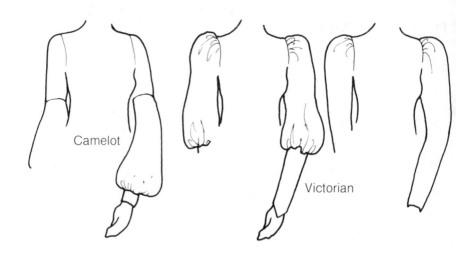

Camelot

Victorian

Back Interest Detail

Interesting Closures

Button/Loop

Fabric
Rose

Outline Yoke Detail

Bow

Lace/Trim/Ruffles on Train

Traceable Veils

Combine
veil with frame or
hat on pages 113
and 114.

Facial/Madonna/Blusher

Ballerina/Waltz/Elbow Length

Fingertip Length

Cathedral Length

Chapel Length

Trains

Trains and bridal veils definitely give your gown back interest. The different types and lengths of trains shown here can be worn with or without a veil (see Chapter XIV).

For formal weddings, we recommend long veils and chapel, cathedral or sweep length trains.

Extended trains are part of the gown design. Detachable or "panel" trains are separate from the gown and attached in the bodice area.

Chapel-extended
or detachable
(for bride and/or
bridesmaid)

Cathedral-extended
or detachable
(for bride only)

Sweep-extended only
(for bride only)

A Few Words to the Wise About Bridesmaid Style Decisions:

• Don't make design and fabric decisions by committee. After you've chosen two or three alternative styles, show them to your attendants. Get a consensus of their opinion, but ultimately you should decide.

• Try to be flexible. Unfortunately we've seen lots of unhappiness come from disputes over pattern and fabric choices. Sometimes conflict can be minimized if the bride pays for part or all of the bridesmaids' gown costs.

• Have all the dresses made by one person — this is the only sure-fire way we know of to make dresses that look alike. If not, the bride should closely supervise all sewing, to make certain that all techniques and fitting are consistent.

• Double-check the final look, fit and hems of gowns one week before the wedding, so there'll be time to make changes.

Other Style Considerations: Convertibility

While some brides would rather store away their dress as is, for an heirloom, some brides (and most bridesmaids) would like to get lots of mileage out of their wedding costume.

You may want a wedding gown that is convertible to simply a more comfortable reception/dancing dress. Or, you and your attendants may want convertibility to a more functional dress later. Here are some ideas:

Removable underskirt   *Removable lace capelet/train*

Also:

Removable bolero/jacket

Removable capelet/shawls

Lace blouse over camisole dress

Two piece — skirt/blouse outfit

Detachable train

Detachable tiers

Overdress or pinafore worn over basic dress

Shortening skirt length

Lace trim can be attached with removable basting stitch. Instantly you have a more casual gown!

V.
Making
Color Decisions

For the bride:

Yes, white still is the most popular choice for brides today. Throughout history white has been a "sacred" symbol of purity and joy. But it wasn't until Anne of Brittany married Louis XII that white was established as the traditional bridal color. Previous to that, red, as a symbol of gaiety, was the norm. The Spanish carried on a tradition of black wedding gowns. Early American women wore their best dress regardless of color.

Anyway, as we said, white is still the choice of most brides today. But "white" comes in dozens of shades—true white, ivory, candlelight, cream, etc.

For most lighter-skinned brides the softened shades are more flattering to their skin tones. The starkness of true white is worn best by darker-skinned brides. If you had your heart set on a *white-white* gown—either try on a few or drape the fabric next to your face—you may look great in it! Different textures of white may be more or less flattering to your face and figure. Satins, for example, will reflect the most light, whereas a textured lace absorbs light.

And don't disregard pastel tints. . .the softest yellow, blue, pink, mauve or grey. Again, they are appropriate (if in the right style) for all the wedding types and can be more flattering than stark or off-white.

For more casual weddings, particularly those we categorize as Updated/Contemporary or Garden/Country Look (see pages 19 and 20),think about colors and/or prints. Gail's wedding gown was blue and an off-white organza print with tiny mauve (her favorite color) flowers, in a border design.

Ask these questions of your fabric color choice:
1) *Will this color flatter my skin tone and figure?*
2) *How will my color choice blend with the bridesmaids'attire and the flowers?* (See following section.)
3) *Will I be able to find trims and laces to blend or match?* (Even whites can be difficult.)

For the attendants/ushers:

At one time custom was to have the entire wedding party dress alike to disguise the bride and groom from potential enemies. That tradition has evolved to one of costumed attendants who are the couple's near and dear friends or relatives and who assist before, during and after the wedding.

Your color and style choices for your attendants are the basis for the truly beautiful wedding and photographs. Above all, you and your groom are the focus for the wedding and shouldn't be outdone by the bridesmaids or ushers. Of all the weddings we've sewn for or consulted on, our recurring criticism was "too much, too loud, overdone."

Here's a checklist to make it really simple to decide on attendant dress colors and prints.

What looks good on Slender Sal might not beautify Bigger Betty.

- Think in terms of the number of bridesmaids or ushers. A bold print or shade might work well for one attendant — yet be too overpowering multiplied by eight!

- Consider the size, or size range of your attendants. Muted or darker shades will minimize a fuller figure.

- Coordinate the bridesmaid and usher attire to the flower scheme.

- "Rainbow" colors (light to dark shades of the same color or actual "rainbow" color differences) are popular . . . make sure the color range is not too drastic among attendants. This can cause considerable visual confusion. Another disadvantage of the "rainbow" effect — it can be distracting when the largest figure is in the most eyecatching color.

- Visualize the wedding photo backdrop — the church, chapel, house, garden, etc. — will it enhance your color choice?

The All-White Wedding

Some brides want "all white" weddings (the entire party dressed in white) and they can be lovely.

We think the all-white party looks best when staged in a colorful garden setting.

Color Focus: Coordinating Your Fabrics and Flowers to a Season

Fabrics can very well "say a season" through their color, texture and weight. Choosing the right fabric for the season of your wedding will not only enhance the look and style of the ceremony but will prove to be practical as well. For example, velvet not only looks unlike a summer wedding, but it would also be hot and uncomfortable.

Usually your fabrics and flowers are the most colorful elements in your wedding, so you will obviously want to coordinate them. Some brides will change their fabric choice because they have a definite flower in mind that doesn't match! Flowers too have color, texture and best yet — scent! They are an integral part of most weddings, even small, intimate ceremonies.

Although most wedding flowers are available year 'round, you are going to pay more for flowers out of season. Flowers can be as expensive as they are lovely . . . blend inexpensive flowers in season with your own personal preferences. Let your florist assist you in the appropriate choice for the dresses, church and reception.

AND, don't disregard dried or artificial flowers . . . they are not expensive, but can be saved for years and have a special, nostalgic look. And by the way, Karen opted for potted plants that she could use as house plants later! Gail chose "wiltless" silk azaleas.

SEASONAL FABRICS & FLOWERS

Spring

Fabrics:
peau de soie
polyester silkies
*crepe — light to medium weight
crepe de chine
*knits — jersey and interlocks
*Qiana® knits and wovens
sheers — chiffon, georgette,
  organza, gauze, voile
cottons — polished, eyelets,
prints
**lace — lightweight, all-over
  types like Chantilly

Flowers:

Acacia	*Daisies
*Carnations	Iris
Daffodils	Violets
Green Ivy	Rubrum Lillies
*Roses	*Stephanotis
Statice	Sweetheart Roses
Tulips	Cala Lillies
Gardenias	
Narcissus	
Cymbidium Orchids	
*Mum varieties	
Anemone	
Phalaenopsis Orchids	
*Baby's Breath	
*Chrysanthemums	

Summer

Fabrics:
polyester silkies
*crepe — lightweight
crepe de chine
*knits — jersey and interlocks
*Qiana® knits and wovens
sheers — all types
cottons — polished, eyelets,
  prints, gingham,
  seersucker
**lace — lightweight, all-over
  types like Chantilly.

Flowers — the same as
spring flowers plus:
Tiger Lillies
Protea
Fuji Mums

*Seasonless fabrics
and flowers.

**Appliqués can be cut
from all lace types.

Autumn

Fabrics
silk worsted
satin
peau de soie
brocade
taffeta, moire'
*crepe — medium to heavy-
  weight
*knits — interlocks and light-
  weight double knits
*chiffon
*Qiana® knits and wovens
velvet — velveteen — velour
  (late autumn only)
**lace — all types

Flowers
*Baby's Breath
*Carnations
*Daisies
*Pom Poms
Statice
Bird of Paradise
*Chrysanthemums
Green Ivy
*Roses
*Stephanotis
dried flowers
*Mum varieties

Winter

Fabrics
silk worsted
satin
peau de soie
brocade
taffeta, moire'
*crepe — medium to heavy-
  weight
*knits — interlocks and light-
  weight doubleknits
*Qiana® knits and wovens
*chiffon
velvet — velveteen —
  velour — corduroy
**lace — especially the heavy,
  re-emboidered types

Flowers
*Carnations
*Daisies
Poinsettas
*Baby's Breath
*Chrysanthemums
Holly
*Roses
*Stephanotis
*Pom Poms
*Mum varieites

VI.
Customizing Fit

Fitting — It's Easier Than You Think

Fitting should be your next step after buying patterns and fabric. In this chapter, we'll show you how to combine patterns and some simple fitting techniques.

You'll be surprised — fitting bridal wear is one of the easiest types of fitting there is . . . the skirts are long and full, so the main fitting areas are the bodice and sleeve sections.

Taking Bust Measurements — Determining Pattern Size

Select the pattern(s) by your bust measurement. If you are between sizes, buy the smaller one. By the way, do not use ready-made bridal gowns as size guidelines. Gail was very proud she could squeeze into a size 10 wedding dress but wouldn't dare buy a size 10 pattern!

If you are full busted (larger than B cup bra size), then take two bust measurements:

Regular Bust _____ inches (A)

High Bust _____ inches (B)

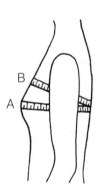

If the regular bust measurement is 2½" or more larger than the high bust, buy the pattern according to your high bust measurement (B). Alter for a large bra cup if necessary (see page 48).

Minimal Wearing Ease

Patterns are designed with built-in comfort — a feature known as "minimal wearing ease." Wearing ease is the extra fullness added to a pattern so that you can move, sit, walk and lift comfortably. Depending on the garment style there may also be additional ease added called "design ease" — it determines the silhouette and fashion look.

When filling out the "Fitting Adjustment Chart" you'll notice a "minimal wearing ease" column . . . we encourage you to add this ease to your body measurements before cutting out the pattern. Later, in the pin-fitting process, unwanted ease can be taken out if you prefer.

Buy Your Pattern(s)

Choose one pattern in your size that has the desired silhouette and hopefully many of the design features you've sketched on the "Traceable Bride". Buy additional patterns to modify the basic silhouette. In bridal patterns look at the unadorned alternate view to really see what the gown looks like. And don't limit yourself to bridal patterns. Page through the entire catalogue. There's certain to be an appropriate style that need only be lengthened. And don't overlook separates — blouses and skirts . . . in the right fabric they can be elegant and are convertible to wear after the wedding.

Combining Patterns

We know how frustrating it can be to search and search for just the right dress pattern. And just when you think you've found it — "Drat! It has a straight rather than full bishop sleeve." Chances are all the design features you've sketched in your "dream gown" are not going to be found in one pattern. So combine patterns!

Pattern companies have standardized their sizing, which makes this process quite easy. Simply combine the patterns you'll need to make your gown. Always buy the same size. Do not mix "for knits only" patterns with those that are suitable for all fabrics.

Karen has experimented with combining patterns and found very little difference in armhole sizes, sleeve cap dimensions, etc., among the same size and similar style patterns from the major companies.

After you've purchased all the necessary patterns, take out the pieces from each that will be used in the gown design. Overlay the pattern pieces and compare, seam to seam, those pieces from the different patterns that will be sewn together. Redraw new seamlines as necessary:

Changing Sleeves

Any sleeve style on pages 35 and 36 can be set into any basic bodice armhole as long as the same size patterns are used.

NOTE: When interchanging sleeves, notches and dots may not match.

Changing Necklines

DON'T FORGET TO ADD SEAM ALLOWANCES.

Compare bodice fronts and backs, matching center front and back seams. Slide pattern up and down until shoulder seams intersect. Redraw the new neckline and shoulder slope on the bodice pattern. Use facings from the neckline pattern.

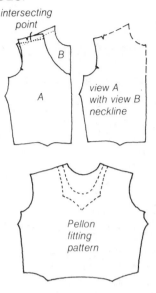

intersecting point

B

A

view A with view B neckline

NOTE: Undecided about which neckline is best for you? Transfer more than one neckline shape to the Pellon Fitting Bodice (see pg. 49). Then as you're trying on the bodice, starting with the highest neckline, cut away until the shape is just right! And remember, you'll have to redraw facings accordingly . . . don't forget those seam allowances.

Pellon fitting pattern

Easy Steps to A Good Fit

1. Pin Fit or Flat Pattern Measure the tissue pattern and record body and pattern measurements.

To Pin Fit the Pattern: Trim excess tissue from the main pattern pieces, lightly dry press and pin in darts. Pin in bodice and underarm seams. You may need to clip into neckline or armhole. Try on the bodice "half-pattern," seam allowances out, over your bridal undergarments, aligning center fronts and back. Check for adequate width and length at this time. Make any notes on the pattern.

Let out or take in the pattern as necessary. Also, check to see that the bust darts are pointing to the point of the bust and are 1″ away from the bust apex. Mark new seamlines.

Note the armhole height — and how much too low or too high.

The shoulder seam should be in the center of the shoulder

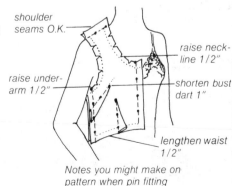

shoulder seams O.K.

raise neckline 1/2″

raise underarm 1/2″

shorten bust dart 1″

lengthen waist 1/2″

Notes you might make on pattern when pin fitting

Pin the sleeve in place at the shoulder seam and underarm. Pinch the pattern in the upper arm to check for wearing ease (1″ pinch = 2″ ease) and sleeve length.

Pin the skirt to the bodice and check for adequate width and length.

To Flat Pattern Measure: Record your figure and the pattern measurements, then adjust the pattern following our easy steps. The notes that you've made during pin-fitting will double-check these flat pattern measurements and alterations.

And if you've never taken body measurements or made pattern adjustments before, we highly recommend reading *Painless Sewing,* by our publisher, Palmer and Pletsch.

Fitting Adjustment Chart

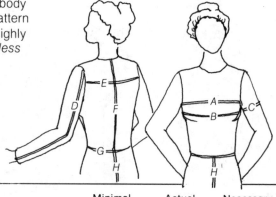

Measurement	Your Measurement	Minimal Wearing Ease	Actual Pattern Measurement	Necessary Alteration* (+ or −)
A. Bust (high)	_____		_____	_____
B. Bust (regular)	_____	2½″-3″	_____	_____
C. Arm Girth (fullest part)	_____	2″-2½″	_____	_____
D. Arm Length	_____	(add hem allowance)	_____	_____
E. Back Shoulder Width	_____		_____	_____
F. Finished Back to Waist Length	_____	¼″	_____	_____
G. Waistline (tummy)	_____	1″	_____	_____
H. Waist to Hem Length	_____	(add hem allowance)	_____	_____
I. Hip (fullest part; Measure at same spot on you and pattern)	_____	2½″	_____	_____
Individual figure problem:	_____	_____	_____	_____

Shoulders:
narrow ____ broad ____ sloping ____ square ____ Back: narrow ____ broad ____

Neck: short ____ long ____ Bust: small ____ large ____ low ____ high ____

*divide total by
number of seams.

2. Make Necessary Pattern Alterations

Bust Alterations (standard pattern cup size is a "B")

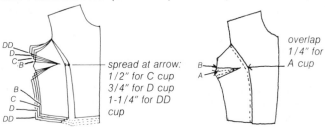

DD
D
C
B

spread at arrow:
1/2" for C cup
3/4" for D cup
1-1/4" for DD cup

B
C
D
DD

overlap
1/4" for
A cup

B
A

Increase Cup Size   Decrease Cup Size

Neckline Alterations   ## Waistline Alterations

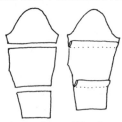

Raise   Lower

Increase Size   Decrease Size

Sleeve Alterations

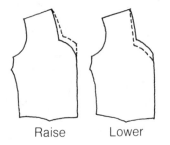

Lengthen   Shorten

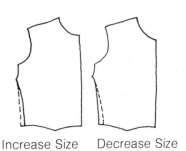

Lengthen   Shorten

Increase   Decrease
Girth   Girth

3. Make an Easy Pellon Fitting Bodice

To ensure a good fit for the bride in the bodice/sleeve areas, we recommend making a duplicate pattern out of Featherweight Pellon® (not fusible).

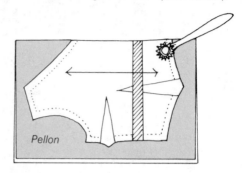

Cut out the Pellon pattern pieces using the altered tissue patterns, but add 1″ rather than ⅝″ seam allowances. Transfer all pattern markings, including seamlines and grainlines, to the Pellon pattern with a tracing wheel and tracing paper.

(In case you're wondering why we don't suggest muslin, here are three great reasons: 1. It shrinks 2. It wrinkles and distorts when pressed 3. It doesn't look like a wedding gown!)

Pellon doesn't tear or ravel and can easily be sketched upon, cut and taped back together.

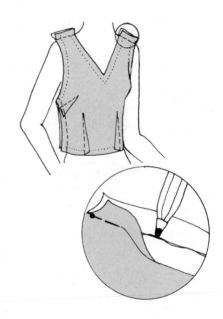

Pin fit or machine baste seams and darts, *wrong sides together*, in the Pellon pattern. Try on the bodice. Make necessary adjustments and mark all alterations with washable marking pen. Remove basting stitches after marking.

We don't stress cutting a Pellon Fitting Bodice for attendants, except for those with dramatic fitting problems. Most bridesmaids we've known neither can nor want to spend the time a bride does perfecting fit.

49

4. Common Fitting Problems and Alterations. Here are some of the common fitting problems that can be solved during the Pellon basic fitting and in your final garment. (try on right sides out)

NOTE: For bridesmaids, these adjustments may be made while pinfitting.

Body Area	Problem	Solution

Bust

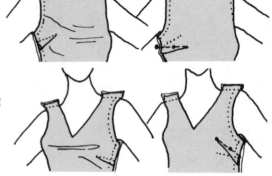

•Low Bust

Repin the dart, pointing it down to the bust point

•High Bust

Repin the dart, pointing it up to the bust point

Shoulders

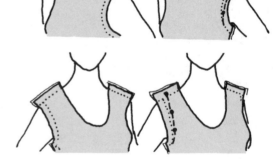

•Broad Shoulders

Pin-mark a narrower armhole seamline, tapering to the original seam at the underarm notch.

•Narrow Shoulders

Pin-mark a wider armhole seamline, tapering to the original seam at the underarm notch.

•Sloping Shoulders

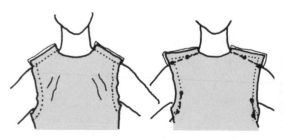

Pin out excess fabric at the armhole edge of the seam, tapering to the original seamline at the neckline. Lower underarm seam the same amount shoulder was lowered.

50

Body Area	Problem	Solution

•Square Shoulders

Let out shoulder seam at armhole edge and taper to original seamline at neckline. Raise underarm seam the same amount as shoulder was raised.

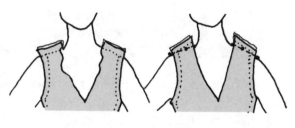

Neck

•Neckline "Gaposis"

Pin out the excess fabric on the neckline edge of the front shoulder seam, tapering to the original seam at the armhole.

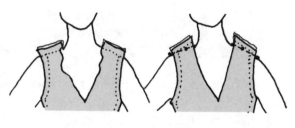

Back

•Broad Back

Pin-mark smaller seam allowances along center back, side and armhole seams.

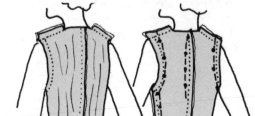

•Narrow Back

Pin-mark larger seam allowances along center back, side and armhole seams.

Armholes

•Tight and/or High Armhole

Pin-mark a deeper underarm seam, tapering to the original seamline at the armhole notches. If necessary, let out shoulder seams as instructed for square shoulders.

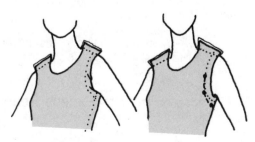

Body Area	Problem	Solution

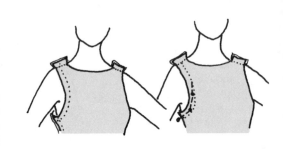

•Armhole "Gaposis"

Pin-mark a narrower underarm seam, tapering to the original seamline at the armhole notches. Side seams may also need to be taken in at the underarm seam.

NOTE: This problem may be caused by a tight bustline...let out side seams and see if the problem is solved.

After fitting the bodice, set in the sleeves, wrong sides together.

Upper Arm

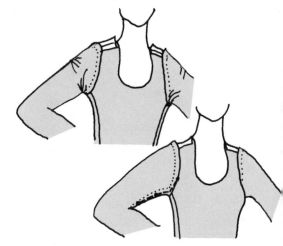

•Large Upper Arm

Let out sleeve seam, tapering to the original seam at the elbow. Pin-mark a narrower sleeve underarm seam, tapering up to the original seamline at the notches. The bodice underarm seam may need to be lowered to accommodate the larger sleeve.

5. Cut, Sew and Fit the Fabric. Use the altered Pellon pattern pieces as your pattern. The 1″ seam allowances are an additional fitting "insurance policy" that will compensate for fabric variances, errors in measuring, last month weight gains, etc.

Sew the gown by sections, fitting the bodice and sleeve sections first and then sewing them to the skirt. Garments should hang at least a day before hemming.

6. After finalizing fit, **Trim Excess Seam Allowances** making them even throughout.

What to Look for in a Good Fit

Check from the side, front and back . . . wear the proper undergarments and your wedding shoes for all fitting sessions.

Front

*Neckline lies close to the body, not gaping

*Smooth fit across sleeve cap

*No pull lines or wrinkles across the bustline

*Darts point to the fullest point of the bust

*No drag lines across tummy area

*Skirt falls smoothly over hips

*Hem is even and a flattering length

Back

*Armhole seam is a smooth curve has no puckers or pulls

*No pull or drag lines across back

*Center back closure not over-strained

*Undergarment lines don't show through the gown bodice

*Snug but not tight fit through waistline

*Train hangs straight and walks easily without cupping under or restricting movement

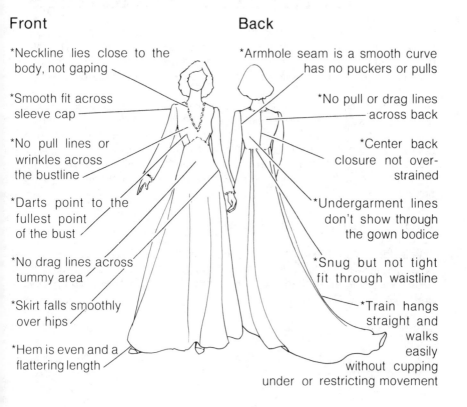

VII. Beautiful Fabrics Make Beautiful Weddings

No doubt after attending a wedding, friends have asked you, "How did the bride look?" How that bride, and you will look, depends largely on the right style and fabric choices, plus of course, construction of the gown. You're in control of all these factors when sewing your own gown.

Refer to the back of the pattern envelope for general fabric suggestions ... but don't let these pattern envelope recommendations limit you — there are dozens and dozens of fabrics available that could be flattering to your silhouette and figure. Some of the loveliest brides we've seen have chosen unusual fabrics, from drapery brocades to tablecloths. Whatever fabric(s) you are considering, please run through our "Fabric Quality Checkpoints" before buying.

Fabric Quality Checkpoints

Quality fabrics are the key to sewing and making a beautiful gown. There's just no sense in wasting time and money on poor quality fabrics that will wrinkle excessively, hang crooked, bag out of shape, "crock" dye on you and your undergarments, etc.

The checkpoints listed below will help you judge whether or not to buy a fabric:

_____ Squeeze the fabric in your hand .. does it wrinkle? A lot? If you or your bridesmaids will be sitting or travelling any length of time, wrinkling could be a problem.

_____ Are there any obvious fabric flaws, fade lines, runs, etc.? Long gowns need several yards of fabric . . . permanent center fold crease lines can be a problem with larger pattern pieces.

_____ If the fabric is a horizontal print, is it "on grain"? If not, it will be difficult to cut out and possibly will not hang well.

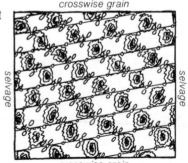

crosswise grain

selvage

selvage

Fabric printed off-grain

crosswise grain

_____ Is there enough fabric? Don't try to mix dye lots . . . they can vary considerably, even "white" shades. Buy all your fabric from one bolt. It's better to buy more fabric than you need, while the fabric is available. When you find attendants' fabric, also have it cut in one piece from the bolt. Always inspect for color differences under bright natural light.

_____ Is the fabric wide enough in relation to the pattern sizes? 36" wide fabric can require lots of time-consuming piecing in a full-skirted gown or in long extended trains.

_____ What is the fabric care code? If washability is a factor, remember to buy washable linings and trims.

_____ Can you find coordinating trims and linings? This may discourage you from choosing a certain fabric or shade. How will the colors blend with your flower choice(s)? With your ushers' attire?

_____ Drape the fabric on you (or your attendants). Will the fabric lend itself to your desired silhouette and wedding type?

Be Honest About Your Sewing Ability

If an experienced dressmaker is sewing for you or your attendants, easy sewing shouldn't be a concern. But, if you or your bridesmaids will be sewing your own, heed the voice of experience. Sewing for a wedding is not the time to learn . . . choose gown styles and fabric you can handle. We know you'll be a whole lot happier (and so will your attendants) while you're sewing and with the finished gown.

Often we've seen an aspiring but inexperienced seamstress/bride try to tackle yards and yards of chiffon or rayon velvet. Either fabric, when handled properly, can be elegant, but in the hands of a beginning or rushed seamstress, watch out!

Knits, medium-weight crepes, cotton blends or cotton laces, can be good choices if sewing ability and time are minimal. Ask the sales consultant at your favorite fabric store about the fabric you've chosen, and how easily and quickly it will cut, sew and press.

This chart, which highlights the handling and use characteristics of common bridal fabrics, will assist you in making selections:

Characteristics of Bridal Fabrics

FABRIC TYPE	SEWING/HANDLING

Delicate Surfaces

Silks Polyester silkies Satin — all weights Peau de soie Brocade (36-50" wide)	• Moderate sewing ease • Snag-sensitive surface • One-way nap and yardage layout • Stitching lines show if ripped out • Heavy fabric may not ease well into sleeve caps • Avoid over handling, over pressing • Check care code
Taffeta Moire' (45-50" wide)	• Moderate sewing ease • Can slip when sewing • Set iron on low temperature • Economical underlayer for sheers, lace • Can be difficult to ease into sleeve caps • Fit should not be tight • Dry clean only
Crepe (45" wide)	• Moderate sewing ease • Slips when cutting • Steam may cause puckers • Fit should not be tight • Check care code

Knits

Stretchy
  Tricot, Jersey
Moderately stretchy
  Interlocks
Stable
  Lightweight doubleknits
(54-60" wide)
	• Easy and quick to sew
	• Easy to fit
	• One-way layout
	• Interlocks can run and require special handling
	• No special sewing machine required
	• Generally washable — check care code

- Traditional wedding gown fabrics
- Soft types used for draped styles
- Heavier types used for sculptured shapes like the princess silhouette
- "Walks" well — good for extended trains
- Use as a background for lace, trims, sheer overlay

- Available in a wide variety of weights, colors, patterns
- "Rustle" sound when you walk
- Very prone to perspiration stains and water spots
- Fingernail polish remover will dissolve fabric if acetate

- Drapes well
- Good for figure camouflage
- Popular for attendants' gowns
- Combines nicely with all-over laces like chantilly
- Available in many fiber types — primarily 100% polyester however.

- Excellent choice for attendants', mothers' gowns
- Easy care
- Drapes well
- Woven jackets, vests, etc. can be added for a more tailored look
- Available in all fiber types — most common are polyester and Qiana® nylon
- Delaine® and Maracaine Q® by Blue Ridge Winkler are lovely

Sheers

Crisp
  Organza, voile,
   nylon sparkle
Soft semi-sheers
  Dotted Swiss, organdy,
  dimity, handkerchief
  linen, gauze
Filmy
  Chiffon, georgette,
  lightweight tricot
(generally 45" wide)

- Sewing ease ranges from easy to difficult
- Can be slippery to handle
- Self fabric used for bindings, facings, interfacings
- Inner construction must be neat because it shows through
- Over-handling should be avoided
- Check care code

Informal Fabrics

Cottons and cotton
blends
(generally 45" wide)

- Easy to sew
- Easy care — may need more pressing if 100% cotton
- Extra yardage required for cutting border prints
- Generally washable — check care code

Napped Surfaces

Velvet
Velveteen
Velour
Corduroy
(36-60" wide)

- Moderate to difficult sewing ease
- One-way nap layout and yardage
- Stitching lines show if ripped out
- Synthetic types can slip when sewing
- Special pressing methods
- Generally dry clean only

Lace Yardage

Yardage
(9", 18", 36", 45", 54",
60", 72" wide)
Trim
(1/4"-6" wide)

- Easy to moderate sewing ease
- Cut on lengthwise or crosswise grain
- No ravelling or fraying
- Fusible web can be used to attach lace
- Motif placement should be planned before cutting out
- To protect texture, press lace carefully
- Lace patterns need to be studied against a dark background for contrast
- Generally dry clean only

58

- Pattern styles should allow plenty of ease (minimum 8" at hip)
- May use more than one layer
- Used as underdress/slip and lining for all seasons
- Popular for spring and summer weddings
- Look for 120" wide sheers in drapery departments
- Crisp sheers make super reception tablecloths
- Available in natural and synthetic fibers

- Comfortable in hot, humid weather
- Recommended for informal weddings
- Border prints can limit pattern selection
- Popular for both bride and attendants
- Convertible to wearing after the wedding

- Choose simple patterns with few seams
- Good for fall/winter weddings — brides and attendants
- Can add visual "weight" to the figure
- Satin and heavy lace work well as accents
- Velveteen isn't as plush as velvet, but easier to handle

- Unlimited design variation possibilities
- Lightweight lace needs net or other sheer fabric for support
- Embellish lace with beads and pearls
- Less expensive laces can be used as reception tablecloths
- Available in a wide range of fiber types

Recycling An Antique Wedding Dress or Fabric

Whether it's reflecting the current trend in nostalgic clothing or a family tradition, many brides at least consider wearing an heirloom — grandmother's, a great aunt's or her mother's wedding gown. Karen cherishes her grandmother's linen and crochet wedding dress, which is displayed in her sewing room on an antique dress form.

But before opting for wearing an heirloom, read on.

1) Try on the dress carefully (old dresses are fragile). If the gown is too small, you risk problems with enlargement — torn side seams and fabric, wear lines, color change and restyling the silhouette entirely. If there is an underdress, it's easier to restyle just that. Gail once made an all-new, very fitted underdress for an antique lace gown that was a size too big for the bride. The slimmer underdress silhouette was very figure flattering and spared handling of the fragile Venetian lace overdress.

2) Are there soil or water stains? Dry cleaning can be risky, with a good chance of fabric deterioration. You may want to cut out a soiled or stained area, make the dress shorter, sleeveless, etc. or replace with new lace or fabric. Or, attempt to match new lace appliques and trim to camouflage spots and stains . . . but remember there are several "whites" available, from candlelight to ecru. Most older gowns have either darkened or yellowed to a degree. You may need to dye new lace or fabric to match this older, aged look.

> **Dyeing Recipe** (best for fabrics with 50% or more natural fiber content) If you're uncertain about fabric content, ask your dry cleaner. Also, you should expect most fabrics to shrink at least slightly through the dyeing process. **WARNING: Test on a small swatch first! Do not attempt to dye "dry clean only" fabrics.**
>
> *One four quart bowl or pan* (no cast iron please) for the average dyeing batch. *Ten regular tea bags* — you may need more if you're dyeing to a dark tan shade. Pour boiling water over the tea bags until the bowl or pan is about two-thirds full. Let the water cool to lukewarm. Remove the tea bags. Put the fabric or trim into the solution. Keep dunking and stirring the fabric or trim until it's the desired color. Since the color will appear to be a shade darker when wet, allow the fabric to dry. Karen speeds up the drying process by using a blow hair dryer on medium heat. She holds it a few inches away until the section dries. If the color is still not dark enough, heat up the water and add two or three more tea bags to darken the solution. Repeat the previous instructions. Do not rinse the fabric again after the desired color is achieved.

3) Is the dress too short? Brides are taller these days and this is a common problem (5'10" Gail towered over her 5'0" grandma). Either make a longer underdress or slip (a ruffled hem on either walks well).

4) Does the dress seem damaged beyond repair? It might well be, but take heart! Some of the lace or trim can probably be salvaged. Cut out lace appliqués (ask Granny first) and sew or fuse them on the new dress fabric . . . even on the ringbearer's pillow.

A NOTE ABOUT STORING YOUR ANTIQUE GOWN — Most older garments are susceptible to the ravages of light, wood acid and bleach. Store in a clean cotton sheet (don't bleach!). Do not store the gown, unprotected, in a wood trunk or closet. Also, give your gown a chance to "breathe". Every other year, refold in a different manner so fold lines don't become permanent.

VIII.
The Bridal Sewing Basics

You've selected the wedding fabrics. Now you just proceed to sew like usual, right? Wrong. To quote Karen, "With bridal fabrics and fashions, less is better. Less sewing, pressing and handling in general makes a more beautiful gown."

Those words should be your guiding light as you're sewing — most traditional bridal fabrics are relatively delicate and can look worn if handled too much. Bridal wear should be sewn to achieve the loveliest appearance and fit for that one special day . . . inner construction like seam finishing is minimal. Casual gowns made from informal fabrics and convertible to everyday wear need to be constructed more durably.

Fabric Preparation

Roll it up —
After making your fabric selection have the store roll it (single layer) on a long tube to prevent wrinkling and creases. Napped fabrics like velvets can be safely pinned by the selvage to a dress hanger, for a short time.

Cover the fabric with a dry cleaning bag, tissue paper or a clean sheet to store until you're ready to sew. Keep away from coffee, food and kids!!

Pre-Shrink Fabric?
Yes, if you and your attendants plan to wash your gowns after the ceremony; pre-shrink the fabric, lining, trim and notions. Make sure that if one attendant pre-washes her fabric, they all do — this can effect the drapeability and color of the fabric.

For gowns with very full silhouettes, or those with large, extended trains, we recommend dry cleaning even if the fabric is washable. There is just too much yardage to deal with when pre-shrinking and pressing! Plus, some fabrics lose their body when washed.

Getting Ready

- **Sharp sewing machine needles.** Remove those old, dull needles from your machine! For sheers, delicate surfaces: size 9 or 11 needle. For knits, velvets and lace, size 11. (Singer Yellow Band needle helps prevent skipped stitches.) Plan to change needles two or three times for one gown. Don't sew over pins — this dulls needles fast!

- **Thread.** Buy several spools of polyester or cotton-wrapped polyester thread. Use an extra-fine thread for lightweight fabrics. Branded types are recommended to ensure consistent quality.

- **Fine hand needles,** sharps # 9's or 10's. Use for pinning as well as handstitching.

- **Thimble.** We don't want blood on the gown! *Hot tip on how to remove small blood stains:* (Gail learned about it at the bridal shop) For "pin prick" blood spots, try this: Thread a needle with a double strand of thread. Run the thread through your mouth putting a little saliva on the strands. Then push the needle through the spot on the fabric. Repeat until the blood spot disappears! *DO NOT ATTEMPT TO REMOVE BLOOD WITH HOT WATER SPOTTING DETERGENTS, ETC. THEY MAY DAMAGE AND SHRINK THE FABRIC.*

- **Extra fine pleating pins** — a must for lightweight or delicate fabrics. For this special garment buy a fresh new box.

- **Extra long (1½") dressmaker pins** with large heads make pinning laces and napped fabrics really easy (now available in fine diameters for silky fabrics).

- **Sharp shears** and embroidery scissors.

- **Marking tools** — see Chapter IX, for the recommended marking tool for your fabric type. For most dry clean only fabrics use tailors chalk or tailors tacks (silk thread works well). For most washable fabrics use washable markers like Mark-B-Gone™ by Dritz®, Wonder Marker by Traum or Washable Marker by Fashionetics.

- **Transparent press cloth or Stacy's Iron-All® soleplate attachment** for your iron, to prevent scorching.

- **Glue** — used when underlining dress for instant basting and for gluing on pearls. Recommended types available as Sobo® and Velvevette®, both by Slomon's. If the gown or dresses will be washed only, try Unique Stitch®.

- **Glue Stick** — new basting adhesive that will not clog sewing machine needle or stiffen fabric. Great for placement of lace before stitching.

- **Tissue paper** for pattern alterations.

- **Notions** that your pattern requires.

Nice Extras

- **Basting Tape** — for easy insertion of zippers, leaves no pinholes.

- **"Fray-check™" by Dritz®** — a clear liquid used to prevent ravelling. Great for metallics and beaded fabrics!

- **Sharp pinking shears** — nice for seam finishing.

- **Emergency spot remover** — soda water!

- **French Curve** — ruler to true up curved design lines. Used particularly if you are combining patterns.

- **Roller Foot** — use to keep fabric from slipping and puckering ("Even-feed" is another similar attachment.)

- **Clean and Glide®** by Stacy — to remove any fusible residue from your iron's sole plate.

- **Seams Great™ or Seams Saver™** precut tricot strips for seam finishing.

- **Fusible Web** — for hemming and attaching lace to fabric.

- **Steamstress®** by Ostrow — great for velvets, final press on all fabrics.

- **Point Turner** — for turning corners in cuff, waistband, neckline facing.

- **Padded June Tailor Board®** — for pressing seams, detail areas.

- **Clean white towel** — for pressing laces, velvet types, beaded fabrics, etc.

- **Scotch Brand Magic Tape®** — for pattern alterations, hem basting and marking on wrong sides of fabric.

- **Cutting board**

Equipment Preparation

- Oil and clean sewing machine. Sew several test seams to remove excess oil. Machine bed and sewing table should be smooth and snag free. Clean out bobbin area often.

- Clean ironing surface.

- Clean iron soleplate with hot iron cleaner. Test press on a scrap of your fabric to gauge temperature.

- Gather large clean sheets for cutting on and keeping work area clean. If using a white fabric, cover the area with a colored sheet — makes seeing easier.

- Clean hands and work area. No goodies or pets!

- Fill several bobbins of your thread color at once.

- Organize your sewing and pressing equipment in one area.

Timesaving Tips

- Lay out and cut all bridesmaids' dresses at once for uniformity and to economize on fabric.

- Transfer all construction symbols with super fast "snip markings." Cut off notches and snip ¼" into seam allowances.

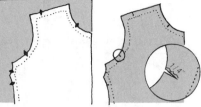

- Mark the wrong side of all fabric pieces with strips of Scotch Brand Magic Tape® — it will be easy to identify right and wrong sides.

- Store smaller pattern pieces in a box to prevent losses.

- Sew on a large table or position an extra table, ironing board or bed behind the machine to hold the large amounts of fabric.

- Try "taut sewing" borrowed from our publisher's bestselling book, *Painless Sewing.* It's instant pucker-prevention for most bridal fabrics! "Pull equally on your fabric in front of and behind the needle as you sew. Do not stretch, just pull taut as if you were sewing with your fabric in an embroidery hoop. However, let the fabric feed through the machine on its own."

- Complete the bodice/sleeve unit before joining to the skirt.

- Hang gown on a padded hanger at least 1-4 days before hemming, to let the fabric relax. We've even tried this hanging technique on long skirt panels before seaming — it helps prevent puckers in knits and medium to heavyweight fabrics. Attach the fabric to a hanger with clothes pins. After it has stretched from hanging, then stitch seams.

- Seam finishing is optional (except on sheers). For a dress you wear only a few hours, why bother?

Pressing

Careful pressing is certainly an important factor in making a beautiful gown. *Do not over-press or over-handle the fabric.* We stress the use of a light-hand press. A gentle up/down motion when opening seams and darts is all that is needed. *Always,* pre-test a sample of your fabric first. Various fabrics respond differently to heat/steam.

"Seal the seam" by pressing in the direction it was stitched, then open it flat. Use fingers and tip of iron to open. *Prevent seam imprint* by pressing over a

seam roll or dressmaker's ham, so the fabric falls away from the seam. Also, place strips of clean paper under seam (an envelope, adding machine tape or notebook paper are convenient). Let seam cool before moving.

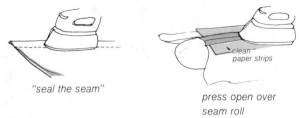

"seal the seam"

press open over
seam roll

Pressing Tips:

- Check fit of gown *before* pressing seams and darts.

- Don't press over pins and basting stitches.

- Don't press the sleeve cap.

- Press waistline seams up.

- Ostrow Steamstress® is a portable steam iron. It can be used for the final press and for pre-wedding touch ups (a favorite pressing aid with us).

Underlinings, Linings and Interfacing

You're right — these aren't the most glamorous fabrics, but as the old saying goes, "beauty comes from within." Underlinings, linings and interfacings are the shaping layers you don't see but do a lot for your finished gown. Some dresses do not require shaping fabrics like these, others are "half-finished" without them. You'll notice on many bridal gowns the bodice is underlined and the skirt is lined.

Underlinings

Fabric Selection

An underlining is cut from the same main pattern pieces as the gown and sewn into the seams. An underlining must be firm enough to shape and support the fabric,or sheer enough to serve as a "background" to support lace. In general, underlinings are used under sheer bodices, or lace, satin and peau de soie fabrics.

Select a soft underlining fabric like Poly Si Bonne® for light support; light to medium non-woven (not fusible) and woven permanent press underlinings for more structured A-line and princess silhouettes.

66

How to Underline

Join the underlining to the wrong side of the gown fabric, pin and glue-baste! Believe it — nothing is faster than this technique invented by Palmer/ Pletsch. Put the two layers together (markings on the underlining layer should be visible — mark construction symbols on this layer only, not the gown).

Lift the fabric back and dab very close to the seam allowance edges, every couple of inches with tiny drops of craft glue (because it dries clear and flexible). Glue around all seam allowances but not the hems. Press with fingers and let dry at least five minutes without disturbing. You may also use glue to "baste in" stitch-in interfacings.

When stitching, treat the two layers of fabric as one! Glue basting will help prevent ravelly edges too. Hemlines won't show if you stitch into the underlining fabric only (use a catchstitched hem, see pg. 96).

Linings

A lining is sewn separately then attached inside the gown at waistlines, armholes and/or neckline seams. Often just the skirt is lined. Fabrics you might line would be sheers, lightweight knits, all-over laces, and napped surfaces. Lining doesn't add weight to the fabric but instead allows the fabric to hang freely while minimizing wrinkles, transparency and clinginess. Lining fabrics range from 100% polyester, rayon and crepe back satin to China silk. Some people recommend taffeta for linings, but we think it "rustles" too much.

How to Line

Cut the basic dress pattern pieces out of the lining fabric. Sew together, making a duplicate of your gown. Press. Place inside the gown, aligning the raw edges of seams as shown, unless your gown is sheer.

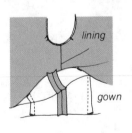

If your gown is sheer, place the right side of the lining to the wrong side of the gown, so the raw edges won't show through. Join the lining to the gown at the waistline seam. Don't bother finishing lining seams — you want them to be as flat as possible. Hem the lining separate from the gown.

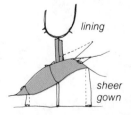

Eliminating Facings

Traditional narrow facings are often eliminated in ready-made bridal wear because they can detract from the sheerness, softness and lightweight nature of the bridal silhouettes. Instead of the standard pattern facings you can line the bodice instead:

1. Lining to the edge. This technique is particularly effective on velvets, laces and metallics. Cut out the lining using the main bodice pieces (sleeves are seldom lined) . . . you will not need the facings.

Right sides together stitch lining and bodice together at armholes and neckline.

Turn to the right side by reaching through each shoulder.

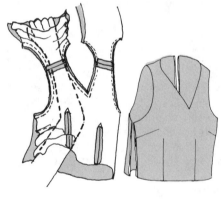

Sew side seams, gown front to gown back and lining front to lining back.

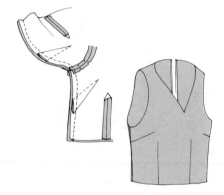

2. French binding: Instead of using facings, you may bind raw edges instead. You'll really like this technique for laces and sheers — any fabric that would be transparent enough to reveal a facing. Karen uses this technique frequently for velvet and velveteen gowns — satin binding looks elegant.

Cut bias strips of lining or self fabric, 2" wide. Fold the strip in half lengthwise and press.

Trim the garment seam allowance to ¼".

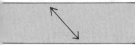  

Pin the binding to the edge, right sides together, keeping raw edges even. Stitch a ¼" seam allowance.

Turn the binding over the seam allowances and blindstitch or machine blindstitch in place.

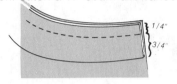 

1/4"
3/4"

Interfacing

Bridal or bridesmaid gowns usually don't have lots of "inner construction" although some lightweight interfacings are necessary to stabilize cuffs, necklines, collars and closure areas.

For sheers, use self fabric for interfacing (try to find the same fabric in a plain color if you're working with a print).

Stacy's Easy Knit® and Pellon's Sheerweight® are soft, pliable fusible interfacings that could be used on many fabrics. Always test interfacings on fabric scraps to make sure they're lightweight enough to gently shape the area. You'll discover as we have that skin-tone beige is more invisible than white.

Fuse interfacings to the facings and upper collars and cuffs. The fused top layer will hide seam allowances and add extra body.

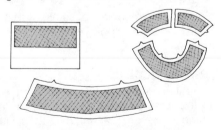

CAUTION: Do not use fusible interfacings on velvets, beaded or any low melt temperature fabrics like taffeta, moire', etc. Use a lightweight, non-fusible interfacing instead like Sheerweight Stitch-in Pellon, Veri-form Durable Press or Armo Press.

IX.
Sewing with Special Bridal Fabrics

Delicate Surfaces—Silkies to Satins

Cutting/Layout

Lay out these fabrics as you would a napped fabric — with pattern pieces in one direction (see page 76). Why? Because the surface luster can cause shading. Use fine silk pins or #10 needles to hold the pattern pieces in place on the fabric. Pin into the seam allowances only. Pins can leave marks on shiny surfaces, particularly noticeable on whites.

For a softer, more comfortable sleeve in heavy fabrics, cut on the bias. Simply fold the sleeve pattern so that the grainline forms a 90° right angle.

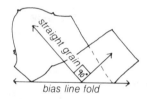

Crease the new fold line. Use it for the grainline when laying out and cutting ... your sleeves will be bias cut. Don't forget to cut a right and left sleeve by flipping the pattern pieces over when cutting single layers.

Marking

"Snip mark" whenever possible (see page 65). Tailor tack with a fine needle. Avoid using a tracing wheel and carbon paper as these fabrics have delicate surfaces.

Sewing Secrets

Try testing seams before sewing your gown. To prevent puckering, try "taut sewing" (see page 65). Adjust pressure on the sewing machine foot to a light setting to prevent marking the fabric with the feed dog. Switch to the small hole throat plate (see page 74).

Use only lightweight synthetic coil zippers. Karen thinks they look best when applied by hand. Use this simple backstitch and a centered application.

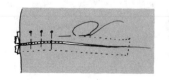

Zigzagging, taping or putting lace on seams to finish is generally not a good idea . . . the seams often show through to the right side. To finish seams, just straight stitch ¼" from the raw edge and then hand overcast, Fray-Check™, or pink the raw edges.

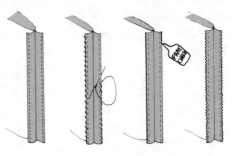

Pressing

Above all, avoid over-pressing. Set iron on a warm/dry setting and press all seams and darts lightly over a well-padded ironing board. Press lightly on the wrong side rather than over-pressing once.

Qiana® Fabrics

Treat Qiana (DuPont's silk-like nylon fiber) fabrics like other delicate surfaces. However, Qiana does require a higher pressing temperature than most synthetics — a low wool/steam is best. Test the iron temperature by trying to set a sharp crease on a scrap without glazing (an overly shiny, melted look) the surface. If the fabric glazes, reduce the temperature. If the crease is not sharp, increase the temperature.

Qiana knits should be sewn with a size 11 needle (Singer Yellow Band if skipped stitches are a problem). If seams are puckering, try this: Stretch seams slightly while sewing. Press the seam. If there are still puckers, stretch the seam, breaking the thread, and restitch.

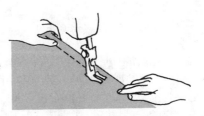

NOTE: Test this technique on a scrap first. In some cases, the fabric may be damaged when the thread is broken.

Knits

Marking

Snip mark and use tailor's chalk. If your fabric is washable, washable marker can be used rather than chalk.

Cutting/Layout

First pre-wash the knit if you will be washing the gown. Warm washing (never hot) and cool rinsing cycles are recommended. Although the amount of shrinkage in synthetic knits may be minimal, pre-washing can remove protective resins that can cause skipped stitches.

Next, determine the "right" side of the fabric — just choose the one you like best! There may be no noticeable difference between the two sides, but you should use the same side consistently as the "right" side.

Press out the center fold. If it is difficult to remove, create a new fold line(s) by refolding the fabric, keeping selvage edges parallel.

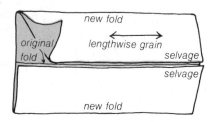

Most knits have at least a subtle nap, since they are knitted in one direction. To avoid possible shading problems, cut out all pattern pieces in the same direction.

Are you using an interlock knit? Interlock knits will run (like your nylons) in one direction when stretched on the crosswise grain. Before laying out your pattern, test cut edges for run direction. Position pattern hemlines so the "runs" run up.

Pressing

Set iron for correct fiber content and press on the wrong side with a press cloth or Stacy's Iron-All® soleplate.

Sewing Secrets

• Pin fit before sewing seams. It is easy to damage knits when ripping out stitches.

• *If you're having problems with skipped stitches,* try these Brown/Dillon sure-fire remedies for this common ailment:

1. Use a new, size 11 "made for knits" machine needle. What seems to cure this problem 99% of the time is Singer Yellow Band Needle (use on any type of machine).

2. Switch to a small hole throat plate (see illustration on page 74). Soft knits tend to be pulled into the larger zig-zag plate opening. Remember, use this plate for straight stitching only.

3. Try "taut" sewing (see page 65).

4. If all the above fail, don't tear out your hair. There's a good chance the machine is clogged with lint and needs a "lube job" — clean and oil thoroughly.

Seams

No seam finish is necessary. But if you're trying to minimize bulk, and the garment is a perfect fit, stitch the seam allowance together 1/4 inch from the first seam line, with a straight or zigzag stitch. Trim to the stitching. This method is particularly useful for run-prone interlock knits.

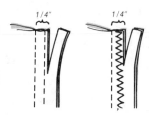

Closures

If you insert a zipper by machine, we recommend Talon Basting Tape® to prevent stretching of the fabric. Buy soft coil zippers for comfort and flexibility.

Sheers

Cutting/Layout

To prevent slippage and make layout easier, filmy and soft sheers should be secured to tissue paper. Fold the fabric in half lengthwise and pin to the tissue. Then position and pin the pattern pieces through all layers.

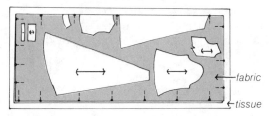

Eliminate facing pieces. Either line to the edge or French bind to finish (see page 68). If you will be putting a double hem in a crisp sheer, allow double the desired hem allowance when cutting. Add an extension to the skirt center back seam if a zipper will be applied to only the lining layer.

NOTE: Double hems are suitable for straight, not flared, skirts.

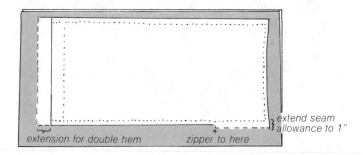

Marking

Carefully! Sheers show everything. Mark with snips or tailor's tacks. Never use dressmaker's carbon or tailor's chalk — both can leave marks that will show through to the right side of the fabric.

Pressing

Test heat and steam on fabric scraps. Pressing temperature will vary with fiber content. Make sure the iron soleplate is snag-free and really clean. Press embroidered sheers face down over a terry towel to protect the texture.

NOTE: Chiffon can shrink when steam pressed. Minimize pressing and use a dry iron at a low temperature.

Fitting

The fit should not be tight. Sheer fabrics are fragile and no strain should be put on the seams.

Sewing Secrets

- To eliminate the need for pinning, lightly baste seams first with Glue Stick close to the seam edges that will later be trimmed away.

- Change to a small round hole plate for all stitching or fill in a zig-zag plate with Scotch Brand Magic Tape®. When the needle goes through the tape, it will form a small hole.

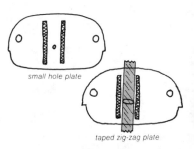

small hole plate

- If the sheer fabric is snagging or slipping, place tissue paper under the seams next to the feed dog — on top the seams too, if necessary. Pull away tissue after the seam is sewn.

taped zig-zag plate

- Use self fabric for interfacing necklines. Choose a plain color if the gown fabric is a print. Organza can be used to interface areas that require more crispness, like closures. Underline the bodice for body, but line the skirt so it will drape. All lining seams should be next to the body, so they won't show through the gown. (see page 67).

Seams

All fitting should be done before the seams are finished. Do not press seams open. Press them together in the direction of the stitching to seal the seam and then press to one side. Seam finishing should be neat since it will show through to the right side.

The Quick Sheer Seam Finish

Straight stitch a 5/8" seam. Stitch again, 1/4" from the first stitching into the seam allowance. Trim close to this stitching. Press seam allowances toward the back of the gown. Fray Check®, sparingly, next to the second stitching (excellent for chiffons). NOTE: Another very quick sheer seam finish is overedging with a serger, a machine now popular with homesewers.

1/4"

The Custom Sheer Seam Finish (also known as the French seam.)

This is a narrow, delicate seam that takes a little more time but the results are worth it. With wrong sides together, stitch a 3/8" seam. Press to one side and trim to 1/8"

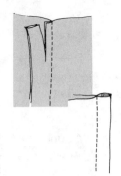

Fold right sides together. Stitch a seam 1/4" from the fold. Press seam allowances toward the back side of the gown.

Closures

Use only the lightest-weight buttons and soft coil zippers. When sewing a zipper into a lined dress, sew through both layers of the underlined bodice, but only the lining of the skirt.

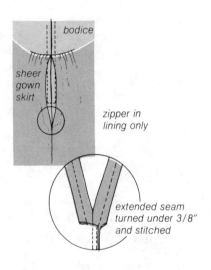

bodice

sheer
gown
skirt

zipper in
lining only

extended seam
turned under 3/8"
and stitched

Turn and stitch seam allowance on the sheer seam edges as shown. If you followed our recommendation and added the extension to this seam when cutting out, it's easier to achieve a neat, finished look on the sheer layer (see page 73).

Informal Fabrics — Cottons and Cotton Blends

Cutting/Layout

These fabrics are a delight to cut out! Be sure to pre-shrink any fabric you plan to launder later. One-way prints should be laid out following the "with nap" diagrams.

Here is an idea for border print or scalloped edge eyelet placement. Pattern pieces should be cut on the crosswise or lengthwise grains. Triple-check hemlines before cutting. Flip pattern pieces to cut both right and left sleeves, etc.

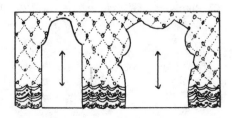

Marking

"Snip mark" and use washable markers.

Pressing

The high cotton content of these fabrics makes them easy to press. However, if they are synthetic blends, be more careful.

Sewing Secrets

When sewing with an open-textured or eyelet fabric, tape over the toes of the presser foot to avoid catching.

Scotch Brand Magic Tape® closes the presser foot toes.

Seams

No special seam finish is required. To minimize ravelling, seams can be stitched and pinked, Fray-Checked™ or stitched and zigzagged (see page 71).

Closures

Buttons fit right into the nostalgic look of these fabrics — button loops are a snap (see our instructions on page 108).

Trims

Informal fabrics are the perfect background for laces, ribbons, rufflings and lace inserts (see page 85).

Napped Fabrics — Velvets, Velveteen, Velour, Corduroy

Cutting/Layout

Determine the direction of the nap by brushing your hand lightly over the surface of the pile. If it feels very smooth, you are brushing with the pile. If you feel some resistance you are brushing against the pile. For the richest color highlights, cut the fabric with the pile running up. For a more muted look, cut it with the pile running down. Whichever method you choose, be consistent when cutting out the pattern pieces, so all the pile runs in the same direction. We guarantee that the shading difference will be very noticeable, not only in your photographs, but during the ceremony as well.

Cut facings from the lining fabrics or line to the edge to minimize bulk (see page 68). Satins and laces are often used for binding and piping . . . cut collars, lapels and cuffs out of them as well.

Since velvet and velour have deep pile, it's best to cut them single layer at a time to avoid slipping and inaccuracy. But take heed from those who have made mistakes — flip pattern pieces to get a right and left side for each garment section. As a safety precaution, Karen cuts duplicate pattern pieces (see page 83).

Pin pattern pieces in the seam allowance. Long pins make pinning easier through thick pile.

Marking
Snip mark and use tailor's chalk or tacks. Tracing wheels will make unsightly marks on pile fabrics.

Sewing Secrets
Make fit alterations before cutting out the fabric. Hand baste darts and seams with silk thread (it comes out easily and doesn't leave marks) before final sewing. Ripping out stitches can damage deep pile.

Sew in the direction of the pile. Practice stitching on a test swatch before starting your garment. Decrease the presser foot pressure to prevent crushing of the pile. Use "taut sewing" (see page 65).

Slash and trim darts to reduce bulk.

Seams
Stitch 1/4" from the raw edge to finish.

Pressing
If you've decided to sew with a napped surface like velvet or velveteen we strongly suggest that you invest in a needleboard or the VelvaBoard® from June Tailor.

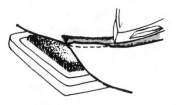

But if you've spent your last dime on the fabric, use a large scrap of velvet or plush towel for your needleboard.

When pressing, place the fabric face down on the "needleboard." Steam darts and seams, lightly finger pressing. Let the fabric cool before moving. DO NOT PLACE IRON DIRECTLY ON THE PILE OR THE WRONG SIDE OF THE FABRIC. Osrow's Steamstress is great because it can steam the seams without fear of crushing the pile — super for touch-ups right before the wedding.

Hang your gown in a steamy shower to refresh the pile. When the gown is not being worn, hang it inside out on a padded hanger to protect the pile.

X.
Making the Most of Laces

Lace is synonymous with weddings — elegant and intricately beautiful. Some brides fall in love with a certain lace even before choosing their gown fabric. But many of the brides we've known have been afraid to sew with laces and unnecessarily so. Sewing with laces is not difficult, just different than sewing with other fabrics more commonly used for everyday wear. So read on and make the most of that special lace fabric!

How Do You Recognize A Lace?

Most laces will be grouped in one area of the fabric store. Always look at lace against a dark contrasting background to see the pattern better. Laces are semi-sheer or sheer and composed of a floral or geometric design motif on a mesh background. Rather than being knitted or woven, laces are constructed with knotted and twisted threads, so either the crosswise or lengthwise grain can be used. The right side of the lace has a pronounced thread outline on the motif pattern.

The Two Main Categories of Lace

Lace is either "domestic" (made in the U.S.A.) or "imported" (made in Europe, primarily France).

Imported laces are generally silk or cotton and re-embroidered with a cord or ribbon outlining the design. They are exquisitely designed with many floral motifs widely spaced on a fine net ground and have a soft, supple hand. Because the re-embroidering is hand clipped between each motif they are costly to produce and more expensive than domestic laces. Imported laces are relatively narrow — 2-6", 9-18" and 36" — so are not used as an "all-over" pattern for a gown, but for motif appliqués, trim and bodice/sleeve areas.

Domestic laces are lovely, but more affordable copies of their re-embroidered counterparts. The designs are more closely spaced, less sheer and not as intricate or as three-dimensional as the imported laces.. Because they are less expensive and come in wider "all-over" patterns (available up to

102" wide), domestics can be used extensively in your gown styling.

Lace Forms—How Lace is Sold

Allover — a wide lace pattern with two straight edges. The motif pattern is repeated over the entire fabric. Allover laces are commonly made of synthetic fibers like polyester and nylon.

Galloon — any lace with both edges scalloped. It's the most versatile of all laces with two or more design strips possible .

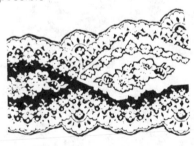

galloon can be clipped apart into design strips and appliqués.

Beading — lace strip with finished "buttonhole type" openings through which ribbon is laced.

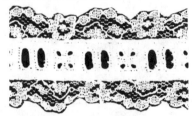

Flounce — has one straight and one scalloped edge, usually 18-36" wide and imported.

Applique — single lace motif design. Can be purchased individually or separated from lace yardage.

Clipped — where the individual lace motifs are separated at regular intervals from one another on the net background.

Sets — denotes the same lace pattern available in several widths. Or "sets" may include the same lace pattern plain (referred to as "flat") and re-embroidered.

Strip — the yardage length of better quality laces, approximately 4½ to 6 yards long.

Trim — narrower laces (up to 6″ wide) available as "edging" (one straight and one decorative finished edge), "insertion" (two finished straight edges used to insert between seam edges or on top), "ruffling" (pre-gathered or pleated) and "galloon" (two scalloped edges). Find in most notions departments in many coordinating lace types and fibers.

Types of Laces

Alencon — *(A-LON-SON)* an imported free-form patterned with a thick satin cord on a fine cotton ground.

Chantilly — a delicate rose pattern with a fine thread outline in a closely spaced design.

Cluny — *(CLOO NEE)* heavy cotton laces with a hand crocheted look.

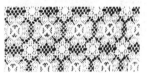

Peau d' Ange *(PO DONJ)* the French word for "angel skin." This type of Chantilly lace has heavier floral patterns and is made with flossier yarn giving it a soft, supple hand. Most often used for appliques.

Venice *(VEN EEC)* is a very heavy open-work cotton lace without a net background. It is easily distinguishable from the other lace types because of its three dimensional look. Widths range from ½″ to 45″. Guipure *(GEE PURR)* and Venice lace are one in the same.

Eyelet — fabrics with cut embroidered design, usually cotton or cotton blend.

Ideas for Using Laces

You too can be as original a designer as Priscilla, Christos or Alfred Angelo! Page through current bridal magazines — often the type of laces are labeled. Select some favorite designs and take them with you to the fabric store. Then study the laces available and how they might be used in your gown design.

Most of the lace types can be purchased in many forms — we've outlined some possible use ideas. Remember, with careful planning, gowns can be adorned using only one yard of lace.

Lace Form	Use Ideas
Allover pattern	• Entire gown design • Bolero, capelet • Camisole • Appliqués — has the most motifs per yard • Bodice/sleeves • Mantillas • Reception tablecloth
Beading (threaded with ribbon, trim)	• Drawstring for necklines, waistline, sleeve cuff • Decorative trim between tiered ruffles • Bodice jabot • Decorative trim
Appliqués	• Accent motif on any part of the gown, headpiece/veil, accessories, etc.
Galloon	• In one piece — as a detachable train, bodice, sleeves, headpiece, trim. • Clipped apart — for veils, hems and necklines. Center motifs can be cut out and used as appliqués.
Sets	• Combine different types in one gown — for example, use the "flat" plain lace for the sleeves, the re-embroidered version for the bodice, trim for the neckline and skirt hem.
Insertion Trim	• Use between seams as a decorative joining (great way to "let out" or lengthen a gown) • Use flat or gather to trim the top of the gown fabric.
Flounce and Pre-ruffled Trim	• Necklines, hems. • Hats.

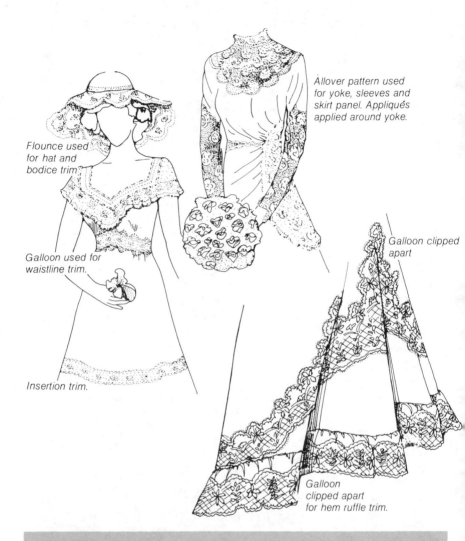

Flounce used for hat and bodice trim.

Galloon used for waistline trim.

Insertion trim.

Allover pattern used for yoke, sleeves and skirt panel. Appliqués applied around yoke.

Galloon clipped apart

Galloon clipped apart for hem ruffle trim.

NOTE: *Lace is never wasted:* sections left over from your gown can be applied to your headpiece frame, the veil, ring pillow or other accessories. We have friends who have saved bridal lace for an heirloom quilt or a baby's christening gown.

Choosing the Right Lace for Your Gown Fabric

Select similar textures and weights. For lightweight fabrics like crepe or crepe back satin, choose Chantilly or Peau d' Ange. For heavier weight fabrics like velveteen or peau de soie, choose Venice, Alencon or Cluny.

Always compare the lace and gown fabric under bright natural lighting to check the color match.

Sewing with Laces

Fit First

Fit before planning placement of lace motifs or sewing. If you've made a Pellon Fitting Bodice (see page 49), transfer all fitting adjustments back to the tissue paper duplicate pattern. You'll need the duplicate tissue to "see through" to the lace design for proper placement and because laces are cut single layer.

To make the duplicate tissue pattern: Buy plenty of tissue paper — enough to make duplicate patterns of all those pieces that will be lace. You will need as many pattern pieces as you have fabric pieces, i.e., two sleeves, and, full pieces for each half piece.

To make a full piece, tape the tissue paper to the fold line of a half pattern piece. Fold the pattern over and trace around the seam edges to outline the other side. For pattern pieces that don't have fold lines, simply cut another pattern out of tissue — mark the right and left on the tissue for easy reference.

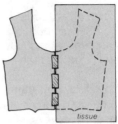

Flip and trace.

Pre-Shrink Laces?

Not usually. Most laces are dry clean only — check the care code. However, if you are adding lace trims or appliqués to a gown you plan to launder later, simply machine wash and dry as you pre-shrink the fabric. Place in a mesh laundry bag to protect the lace.

Lace Layout

When working with laces, layout is the most important step . . . you don't need an engineering degree, but careful planning is a must. Always cut out the lace over a dark surface so the motif pattern will be obvious. Play with the tissue paper pattern pieces until you're totally satisfied with the motif placement (the larger the motif design, the more crucial this placement will be).

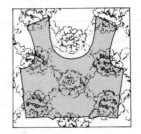

Inspect your lace closely to see if it's a one-way design. If so, cut all pattern pieces in the same direction.

Since laces are textured, regular short pins will get lost. Pin instead with 1½" long, large colored head pins. They're easier to see and handle.

Cutting

Before cutting out your gown you'll need to know how to "clip". First, get a pair of very sharp embroidery scissors. Next, trim around the lace motif pattern, leaving a short "whisker" around the lace (it's not a homemade look — whiskers are seen on $1500 readymade wedding gowns). And don't worry, the lace won't ravel like other fabrics.

Expensive re-embroidered laces will be the easiest to clip because their motifs are clearly outlined in cord. Inexpensive lace and all-over patterns require closer inspection to determine where to cut. Karen devised a clever way to find lace patterns; she cuts open a large, clean trash bag (green or black) and places it underneath the lace layer. The dark color helps define the lace motif and makes it easier to cut.

You will also need to *decide on the seam treatments before cutting.* For all-over lace patterns and those in which the motif pattern is not pronounced, conventional seams as indicated on the pattern are fine, but extend the seam allowances to 1" rather than ⅝".

The other type of seam treatment is called the "lapped" or "invisible" seam. Use this technique when sewing with heavier, re-rembroidered laces, especially on conspicuous seams like yokes, shaped bodices, center backs and fronts, skirt side seams, etc. The seams overlap each other on the same motif pattern, thereby becoming invisible. While laying out the pattern, trace the motif design with thread or on one side of the seam. Use this as a guide for the layout of the corresponding seam. When lapped the two seams should match.

Cut away around motif (larger than tissue) to match back seamline.

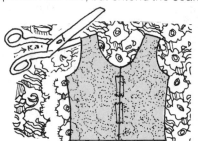

Back is cut to continue motif.

This technique takes longer to layout but the professional look is worth it! Don't take the time to match all seams (it will be difficult to do so anyway) — use conventional seams in less conspicuous areas like shoulders, bodice and sleeve underarms, etc.

After cutting out, mark with tailor tacks and basting thread in a contrasting color. Don't bother with snips and notches — they're impossible to see.

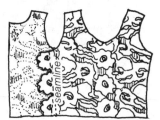

Lap front over back, matching designs. Machine topstitch or hand whipstitch in place.

Machine Stitching

Set your machine at 12 stitches per inch . . . the more open the lace, the closer the stitches should be. If the lace pattern is quite open, you may have problems with the presser foot catching in the mesh. To prevent this, wrap tape around the front of the foot. Sometimes when the lace still keeps getting caught on the foot or feed dog, place tissue paper on both sides of the seam. Tear away the tissue after stitching. Gail regards this as a last resort because it can be time-consuming and she never has that much tissue paper around!

Applying Lace Trims

Sewn in the seam - The lace must be applied during the construction of the gown. For even trim every time, follow these steps:

1. Gather the trim if necessary. (See ruffle technique on page 88.)

2. Sew the trim to the right side of garment piece along seamline as illustrated.

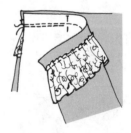

3. Place fabrics right sides together. Pin. Sew the seam, stitching along bobbin stitching line from step 2. Perfectly even trim!

Applied to a finished edge — with right sides together, align finished edges of trim and garment. Whipstitch by hand or machine stitch through both layers.

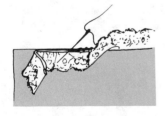

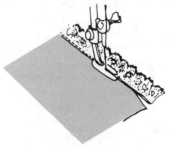

Applied to a raw edge

1. Trim seam or hem to ⅜". Right sides together, stitch the lace trim to the gown. Clip and notch where necessary around curves and corners.

2. Topstitch with a medium width zigzag or straight stitch ⅛" from the seamline through all layers to hold the lace in place. Tack to secure at seamlines.

sew to edge of fabric

turn up and topstitch

Insertion

Position flat insertion trim on the right side of gown fabric. Pin in place. Topstitch over to the edge with a narrow zigzag stitch. Cut away fabric underneath close to the stitching line. This look is seen frequently on Mexican wedding dresses.

Overlapping lace trim — any flat lace can be joined to another piece by overlapping the edges, pinning and stitching.

Join by overlapping the depth of the scallop and straight stitching along the straight trim edge or follow the scallop.

or, for an open airy look, overlap just slightly; straight stitch in place.

We've seen brides overlap lace trim to create the fabric for the sleeves or bodice of their gown — make the fabric first with the overlapping laces and then cut out your pattern pieces.

Applying straight lace to a curved

edge — If you are going to curve a straight trim, choose one with enough detail to camouflage slash marks. Good news — if the curve is slight, you may not need to slash at all. Using your steam iron, try to shape the trim to the curve, stretching the outside edge and easing in the inside edge.

On more severe curves, the lace will need to be slashed. Pin the trim to the edge. Clip into the design *around motifs* at regular intervals where there is excess fabric. Overlap slightly and pin in place.

Again, use your steam iron to curve the lace as much as possible. Stitch to the gown by hand or machine (be careful not to pull the inside edge as you stitch).

Applying straight lace to corners — miter you must! Gail has a nifty
technique that's goof-proof. All you'll need is an iron. At the point of the miter, fold the trim. Bring the folded edge over to the outside edge of the trim, forming a 45 degree angle. This creaseline will be your guideline for stitching. Back-stitch at both ends of the miter seam. Open, trim and press the seam.

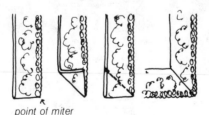

point of miter

Applying beading lace — Weave ribbon in and out of the openings
before applying the lace. Usually beading lace is stitched to a finished edge or seam.

Applying gathered laces — laces can be purchased pre-gathered or you may gather them. When gathering lace, plan on buying at least 2 or 3 times the finished length. Divide the trim and area to which it will be applied into equal sections and mark with pins — it will then be simple to evenly distribute the gathers.

Some flat lace has a heavy thread stitched along the edge which can be drawn up for gathering. Or, using a wide, long stitch, zigzag over a heavyweight thread like buttonhole twist. Secure one end of the heavy thread and pull up the other — this is one gathering stitch that won't break!

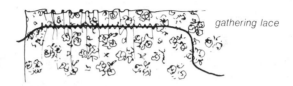

gathering lace

You'll need more gathers around corners. Enclose the gathered edge in a seam (1) or place under a turned seam allowance and hand or machine stitch in place (2).

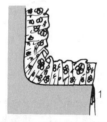 

NOTE: When piecing lace — if seams will show, try piecing trim with French seams (see page 75). Or overlap, camouflaging or matching the lace motif.

Shaping Lace
For a Sculptured Lace Bodice:

This fitted bodice requires shaping of the flat lace to the contour of the bustline. Light to medium weight fabric laces can be underlined with fabric or tulle, but heavier laces need not be. Underlinings can be seamed and darted just like the pattern. However, darts and seams will be eliminated for the lace layer of the bodice by clipping the lace and positioning it to fit the bust shape.

The easiest way to shape the lace to you is on you! Have a friend help you shape it to you or use a dress form. If not underlining, wear a closefitting T-shirt and have her pin the lace to the shirt. Clip the lace close to the motif, overlap to shape.

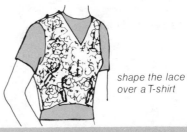

shape the lace over a T-shirt

NOTE: Shape the front bodice first, remove and then fit the back — (or you won't be able to take off the T-shirt).

Align and lap the lace motifs so that the clipping is invisible. Pin and baste to secure. On lighterweight laces, machine stitch the lace in place. On heavier laces, it's easier to hand whipstitch the shaped lace in place. Trim away under layer.

Join at conspicuous seams by overlapping (see page 84) or in "hidden" areas with conventional seaming.

For An All-Over Lace Bodice

- Loosely position pattern pieces (try using weights rather than pins). Avoid placing a large motif at the point of the bust — you don't want the bustline-bullseye look!

- On main bodice sections, the large lace motif should be centered on the center back, center front, middle of the sleeve, etc.

- Sew seams and darts with conventional seaming.

- If the bodice is to have a scalloped hem edge, cut the lace to form the scallops before laying out the pattern. Leftover scalloped edge can be used for cuffs, at the neckline or on the headpiece.

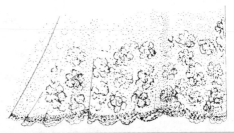

For An All-Over Lace Skirt with a Scalloped Border

NOTE: For this hem style, choose a gown with a straight or just slightly curved hemline.

1. Determine the exact finished hem length. Mark this correct hemline across all the skirt pattern pieces, parallel to the original hemline.

2. Center pattern pieces over the major motifs. Align the center front and back seams perpendicular to the scalloped edge.

3. Align the hemline with the scalloped edge, starting from the center front and back seams and working toward the side seams.

4. If the hemline is slightly curved, clip the lace between motifs from the side seams to the point on the hem where it begins to curve.

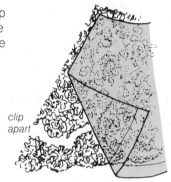

5. Overlap the motifs until the scalloped edge follows the curved hemline. It may be necessary to take tiny snips along the cut edge of the lace so the section will lie flat.

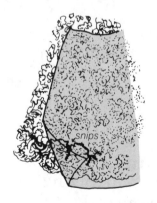

6. First baste re-positioned lace in place and double-check hem length and curve. Then secure in place with hand or machine stitching. On heavier textured laces it's easier to sew laces with a hand whipstitch than by machine.

7. Cut away excess lace below scallop curve. The lace will not match perfectly, but the "seam" will be well hidden in the lace texture.

For Lace Sleeve With or Without Scalloped Hem

- For an all-over lace pattern, cut as you would other fabrics.

- For a scalloped-hem sleeve choose a pattern that has a straight or only slightly curved hem edge.

- Position the sleeve pattern so that a full motif is centered in the middle of the sleeve.

centered
motif

- Since underarm seams are seldom scrutinized, we say stick with the conventional rather than lapped seam.

For Lace Appliqué Hem, Edges, Seams

If the lace doesn't have a scalloped edge, simply appliqué one on! Cut a line of similar lace motifs and appliqué to the edge with fusible web (see following section) or machine stitching (can be straight or a narrow zigzag).

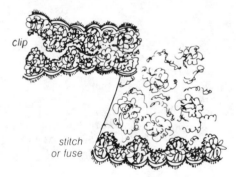

clip

stitch
or fuse

Lace Closures

When sewing a zipper into an all-over lace gown, sew through both layers of the underlined bodice, but only the lining of the skirt (see page 75).

Lace Hems

Horsehair braid is a good hemming technique for all-over lace skirts (see page 95). When lining laces, hem the two layers separately. The lining should be short enough that the scallop pattern (if there is one) shows. Allow the two layers to hang at least overnight before marking the hem. Or, finish a plain edge lace with another lace trim or binding (see French binding on page 68).

Fun Tricks with Lace

- Fusing is a great way to attach lace appliques to your garment. Cut the fusible web about ¼" smaller than the motif size. Sandwich the fusible web between the wrong side of the motif and the right side of the fabric. Double-check the placement. Steam baste the motif in place by holding your iron a few inches above the motif.

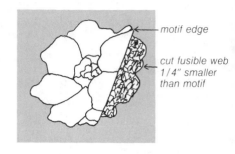

motif edge

cut fusible web 1/4" smaller than motif

Fuse in place following package instructions. WARNING: Test fabric and lace for heat sensitivity before fusing. Use a presscloth or the sticky, melted fusible web will bleed through the lace "open" areas to the iron soleplate.

- Try dyeing cotton or cotton/blend laces (see our recipe for dyeing page 60). Do not attempt to dye wide (45"+) laces because the risk of shading is great.

- Pre-washed laces can be limp. Re-crisp by spraying with spray starch.

- Lace can be hand basted to your gown. Remove after ceremony and use for a christening gown or on a special quilt or pillow.

- To give a "puffed look" to a small flower applique' (2" in size or so), put a small amount of fiber fill between layers before stitching together. A cotton ball can be used as filler in dry clean only gowns.

insert fiber fill or cotton ball

XI.
Hems

Hems are important . . . a beautiful gown can be ruined by an ugly hem. And if a gown is improperly hemmed it won't "walk" well, creating a disturbance all the way down the aisle!

Hemming Hints:

- Most bridal fabrics need to "hang out" before hemming. Allow them to hang at least 24 hours.

- Wear your wedding shoes when marking hems — jogging shoes just won't do.

- Don't add extra bulk to the hem edge by adding tapes, laces, etc. Most hems should be finished with a row of straight stitching ¼" from the raw edge.

- To minimize bulk, layer seam allowances — trim conventional seams in hem allowance to ⅜".

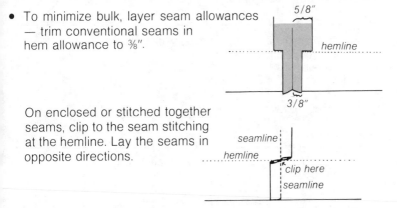

On enclosed or stitched together seams, clip to the seam stitching at the hemline. Lay the seams in opposite directions.

- All the bridesmaids should use the same hemming technique on skirts and sleeves, etc.

- Test all hemming techniques on scraps of fabric.

- The more flared the skirt, the narrower the hem should be:

Hem Depth Guide

Straight-line	2-3"
Princess/A-line	1-2"
Flared	1/2"
Circular	1/4"

Since more than one hemming technique can be used on any one fabric type, we've grouped them together according to suitability.

Fabric	A Guide to Suitable Hemming Techniques

Delicate Surfaces	For heavier weights like peau de soie, brocade, moiré, etc.:
	    Catchstitched
	    Horsehair braid*
	For lightweights like crepe-back satin, crepe, etc.:
	    Catchstitched
	    Machine-rolled
	    Hand-rolled
	    Machine-overedged
	    Lettuce leaf
	
	*Horsehair may be suitable for some lightweights too, especially for gown silhouettes like bouffant, A-line and princess.

Knits	For heavier, more stable knits like doubleknits:
	    Fused
	    Catchstitched
	For softer, lighter knits like tricots, single-knit jerseys, interlocks:
	    Machine-rolled
	    Machine-overedged
	    Lettuce leaf

Sheers	For crisp sheers like batiste, organdy, nylon sparkle:
	    Horsehair braid
	    Double hem
	For soft or filmy sheers like chiffon, georgette, organza, voile, etc.:
	    Machine-rolled
	    Hand-rolled
	    Machine-overedged
	    Lettuce leaf

Informal Fabrics Cottons/ Cotton Blends	For heavier weights like linen-looks, broadcloths, etc.:
	    Fused
	    Horsehair braid
	For lighter weights like gingham, eyelets, etc.:
	    Machine-rolled
	    Machine-overedged
	    Double hem

Napped	Catchstitched for all weights

Lace	For heavier laces like Venice:
	    Horsehair braid
	For lighter weight laces like Chantilly:
	    Hand-rolled
	
	Note: Many lace hems will need no hem finishing because lace does not fray or ravel.

1. Fused Hem

For straight and slightly flared skirts or sleeves, use fusible web for a really quick hem! Flared hems are difficult to fuse because of the excess hem allowance fabric. There's an easy way to get yards and yards of even width fusible strips — a "jelly roll" method made famous by our publishers:

Roll the fusible and snip through the roll at even intervals the desired width. Unroll long, even strips. The strips should be ¼-½" narrower than the hem depth for medium to heavyweight fabrics. For lighter weight fabrics, the fusible strips should be only ½" wide to prevent stiffness.

On most fabrics, you won't need to finish the hem when fusing, although interlock knits should be stitched ¼" from the hem edge to prevent runs.

Press the hem up as marked.
Always press from the wrong side.

Enclose the strip of fusible web inside the hem, ¼" from the raw edge. Steam baste for 2 seconds in each section.

If the hem looks smooth, press 10-15 seconds with a steam iron in each direction. Do not press over the hem edge — this will leave an imprint on the right side.

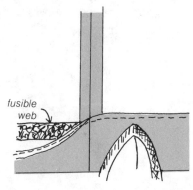

fusible web

NOTE: You will notice that fused hems are a little stiffer than other hem methods. Please test first before using this technique on your gown.

2. Horsehair Braid Hem

Horsehair braid hems are sewn by machine, so they're really quick and easy. The only tricky part of this quick hemming technique is first marking your hem exactly. Once the hem is trimmed it's too late to lengthen, although it can be shortened.

NOTE: If you want a very soft, draped skirt silhouette, don't use horsehair braid . . . it makes the hem "stand out" slightly, defining the silhouette.

1. Lay the horsehair braid ⅛" from the hemline on the right side, as shown. Horsehair braid comes in many widths, up to 6". The most versatile width for bridalwear is 1".

2. Topstitch very close to the edge of the horsehair braid, being careful not to stretch the braid as you sew.

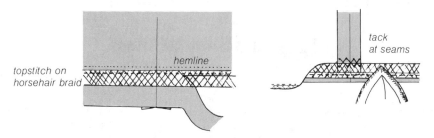

topstitch on horsehair braid

hemline

tack at seams

3. Trim the hem allowance to ¼" and press up the horsehair braid to the wrong side of the gown. Tack the horsehair braid at seam lines.

NOTE: Horsehair hems can "catch" on carpets, especially long trains. Enclose the horsehair with slightly wider width satin ribbon if catching is occurring. Simply topstitch the ribbon on and tack at seam lines to secure.

Satin ribbon encloses horsehair braid that can catch on carpets.

3. Catchstitched Hem

This "invisible" hem is sewn by hand. The flexibility of the stitches prevents pulling on the hem threads and unsightly marks on the right side of the gown.

1. To finish the hem edge, machine stitch ¼" from the raw edge.

2. Using that stitching as a guide and working left to right, catchstitch the hem *loosely.*

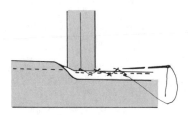

4. Machine-Rolled Hem

1. Trim the hem allowance to ½"

2. Turn up the hem ¼" and stitch in place.

3. Turn the hem up another ¼" enclosing
   the raw edge and stitch in place.

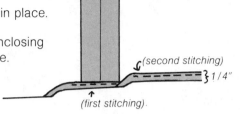

(second stitching)

(first stitching)

³ 1/4"

5. Hand-Rolled Hem

The machine rolled hem may be a little
stiffer than you desire. If so, roll by hand
. . . the look is very soft, like the edge
of a silk scarf.

1. Turn up ¼" and stitch in place.
   Do not press.

2. Turn up another ¼" and blindstitch
   in place.

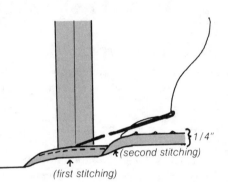

³ 1/4"

(second stitching)

(first stitching)

6. Machine-Overedged Hem

1. Turn up the hem allowance to the wrong
   side.

2. Set your machine on a blind hemming stitch.
   From the right side, stitch along
   the hemline fold edge.

3. Trim the hem allowance to the
   stitching on the wrong side.

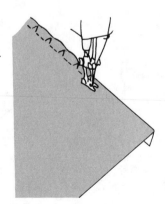

7. Lettuce Leaf Hem

1. Set machine on a medium to wide width, close zig-zag stitch.

2. Fold under the ½" hem allowance to the wrong side.

3. Begin stitching, stretching the edge from in front and back of the presser foot. The more you stretch the edge, the more curl will form.

4. Trim hem allowance to the stitching.

NOTE: Experiment before hemming on a scrap of fabric to determine how much stretching is necessary, the width of the zig-zag, etc.

8. Double Hem

This hemming technique adds weight to a straight hem edge (great for light-weight, sheer fabrics). It shouldn't be used in flared silhouettes like the A-line or princess.

1. Allow double the hem allowance depth when cutting out the fabric (from 4-12").
2. Turn up half the hem allowance to the wrong side.
3. Turn up the same depth again, enclosing the raw edge.

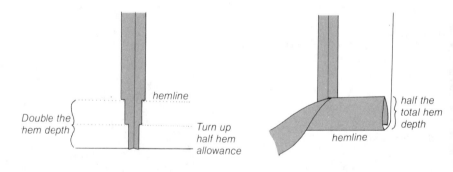

4. Machine topstitch or blind hem stitch the hem. Press.

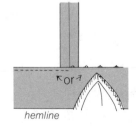

5. Optional — you can cover the stitching line with ribbon, lace or trim.

XII.
Under the Gown

Your gown is not complete without a slip. In fact, a slip is a must for a perfect fit and attractive "walking". It creates a smooth line beneath the gown and prevents the skirt from gathering or bunching up between your legs. Straight-line silhouettes need only a basic long slip, but fuller skirts need additional shaping . . . you'll discover full slips are the most expensive to buy, yet easy to make. Some bridal patterns include sewn-in slips as part of the gown design. We prefer separate slips because they don't add weight or bulk to the gown itself.

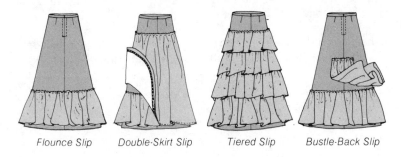

Flounce Slip   Double-Skirt Slip   Tiered Slip   Bustle-Back Slip

Making the Basic Slip

Although there are several slip style variations, each begins as a basic A-line skirt. Use a smooth polyester lining, light satin taffeta or, for the tiered style, medium weight regular Pellon adds extra body.

1. Find an A-line skirt pattern that fits.

2. Using extra tissue paper and a ruler, extend the skirt to full length (slightly shorter than your gown, plus hem allowance).

3. Measure hemline. It must be at least 60" around for easy walking.

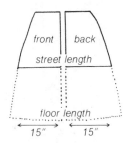

4. Cut the slip out, placing the center front on the fold.

5. Sew the A-line skirt. Bind the top edge rather than finishing with a waistband (see page 68). A zipper is unnecessary — leave the seam open, top stitching the seam allowances down. The fit should be smooth so it won't add any bulk to the gown silhouette or your figure. Sew a hook and eye to the binding for fastening.

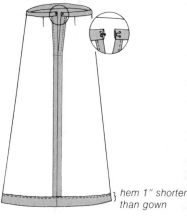

hem 1" shorter than gown

6. Hem the slip 1" shorter than the gown length. Try on with your gown and wedding shoes to check the length.

7. Your basic slip is finished ... it can be worn as is under straight-line gowns, or customized for fuller silhouettes with net ruffles (instructions follow).

The Flounce Slip

The flounce slip is worn with A-line or princess silhouettes. The flounce style skims the hip area, but adds fullness at the hem.

Net Required: 1½ yards of 72" wide crisp net.

1. Make the basic A-line slip.

2. Cut net sections as shown.

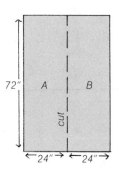

3. Stitch together the short sides of the ruffle with a ½" seam allowance. Press seams open.

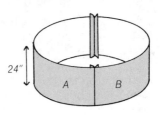

4. Fold ruffle in half lengthwise. Machine-baste raw edges together. Gather the edge using the technique described on page 88.

5. Pin ruffle to the slip, about 13" up from the slip hem. Distribute gathers evenly.

6. Stitch ruffle to the slip with a machine baste stitch. The basting can be easily removed after the wedding.

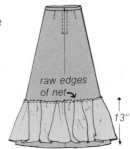

raw edges of net

The Double-Skirt Slip

The skirt style slip should be worn under fuller princess silhouettes and soft gathered skirts.

Net Required: 3½ yards of 72" net

Horsehair Braid Required: 4 yards of 1" wide

1. Make the basic A-line slip.

2. Cut net sections as shown.

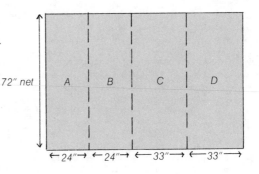

72" net

A   B   C   D

←24"→ ←24"→ ←33"→ ←33"→

3. Make the Flounce slip, as instructed (sections A and B).

4. Stitch together short sides of sections C and D, with ½" seams. Press open.

5. Stitch horsehair braid to overskirt hem edge, ¼" from the edge. Turn up hem and stitch through all layers holding the braid in place.

6. Gather the other edge using the technique described on page 88.

7. Pin overskirt to slip, over bottom ruffle and about 30″ from the basic slip hem. Align the overlayer and slip hems. Distribute gathers evenly.

8. Stitch ruffle to the slip with a machine baste stitch.

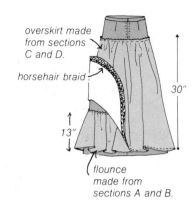

overskirt made from sections C and D.

horsehair braid

30″

13″

flounce made from sections A and B.

The Tiered Slip

The tiered slip is perfect under bouffant silhouettes.

Net Required: 4¾ yards of 72″ net.

1. Make the basic A-line slip.

2. Cut net sections as shown.

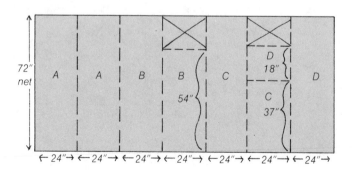

72″ net

| A | A | B | B | C | D 18″ | D |

54″

37″

←24″→ ←24″→ ←24″→ ←24″→ ←24″→ ←24″→ ←24″→

3. Stitch together the short sides of A to A, B to B, C to C, D to D, as shown. Press seams open.

4. Fold the sections in half lengthwise, gather and sew to the basic slip as previously instructed. Position at the indicated intervals.

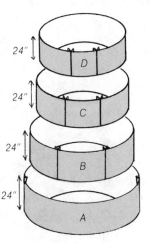

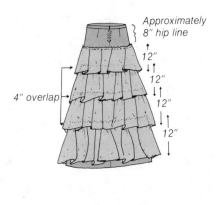

Approximately 8" hip line

12"

12"

4" overlap

12"

12"

We've even seen this slip style made in Chantilly lace — expensive but lovely!

The Bustle-Back Slip

The bustle-back style is of course great for bustled gowns, but works well when worn with extended trains too . . . the net bustle holds the train away from the body.

Net Required: 2¾ yards of 72" net

1. Make the basic A-line slip.

2. Cut net sections as shown.

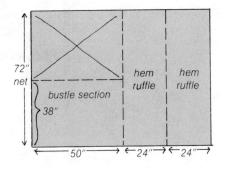

72" net

hem ruffle

hem ruffle

bustle section

38"

50"

24"

24"

2. Fold bustle section in half to form a 38″ × 25″ piece.

3. Gather the 38″ cut edges to 10″ wide.

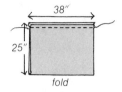

fold

4. Position the gathered bustle over the center back seam, about 26″ from the hem. The net hems should be even with the bottom edge of the basic slip.

5. Machine baste the gathered bustle in place.

Prevent Ruffle Droop

Sometimes the weight of the ruffle can cause the skirt to droop at the waistline seam, especially on medium to heavyweight fabrics. To prevent this, add a supporting ruffle.

1. Cut a 4-5″ wide strip of organdy (or any other crisp, lightweight fabric), 2-3 times the waist measurement.

2. Fold the strip in half lengthwise.

3. Gather the raw seam edges using the technique described on page 88.

4. Pin to the waist seam allowance, distributing the gathers evenly.

5. Machine stitch to the waist seam allowance, being careful that the organdy doesn't interfere with any closures.

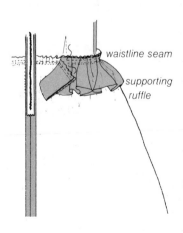

waistline seam

supporting ruffle

XIII.
Easy Finishing!

After studying expensive bridal gowns, we discovered that the fine finishing handwork wasn't handwork at all! Beads and laces can be glued on . . . hems can be machine stitched . . . button loops are from premade trim.

We've put together a collection of some of the fastest and most fun finishing techniques for bridalwear . . . after sharing them with one of our friends she said, "If I knew sewing for a wedding was this fun and easy, I'd get married more often!"

Thank Goodness for Glue

There was a time when a prospective bride spent hours sewing tiny beads and pearls to hand crocheted laces. Let's face it, most of us just don't have that kind of time. But the look of lace appliques, beads and pearls is more popular than ever and easier too now that you can glue. Use a craft glue that stays clear and flexible after drying — SOBO, Quik or Velverette (our favorite because it dries the fastest).

Applying pearls and beads

1. Separate all the pearls or beads into small dishes or a muffin tin. Squirt a glob of glue onto a piece of wax paper.

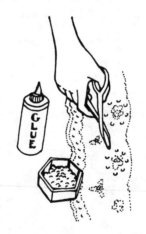

2. Using "scissor style" tweezers, dip the pearl or bead into the glue. Allow it to dry for a couple of seconds.

3. Place the pearl or bead on the lace or fabric. Do not move until the glue has completely dried.

NOTE: This glue application is not as sturdy as hand sewing each individual pearl or bead. But gluing is sure quicker.

Applying Lace Appliqués

1. Mark placements of appliqués on the gown or headpiece.

2. Lightly dot the back of the lace motif with glue. Smooth the glue around with your finger.

3. Apply glue side down to the right side of the gown.

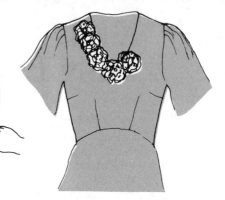

Beading by Hand

Some small beads and sequins must be applied by hand. It's not as fast as gluing but we've found some ways to streamline the process . . . if you're in a hurry, limit the beadwork to small areas. For the speediest outlining, buy prestrung beads. Craft shops have the largest selection of both single and prestrung beads.

1. Plan the beadwork design on your gown (beading is applied after the gown is made). Beads can enhance a lace motif or outline a design on a plain fabric. If beading your own design, draw the motif on a piece of tissue paper and pin it in place over the fabric. The tissue can be carefully pulled away after completing the beadwork.

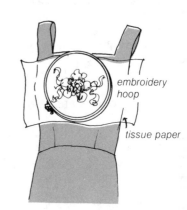

embroidery hoop

tissue paper

2. An embroidery hoop will help keep the fabric taut while you're handstitching. Back lightweight fabrics with underlining to reinforce the design area.

NOTE: Embroidery hoops shouldn't be left on for extended periods of time — they may stretch or distort the fabric.

3. Wax thread with beeswax and use a "beading" needle. The thread should be double and kept short to prevent twisting and knotting. If you pull stitches too tight, the fabric will pucker. Be sure your hands are clean!

beeswax in holder

a. Apply **single beads** with a backstitch.

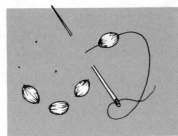

b. **Single beads in outline designs** can be applied by placing two or three beads on the thread and using a running stitch.

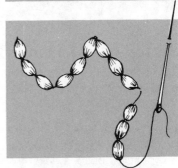

c. **Prestrung beads** are the fastest! Position on gown and whipstitch in place.

d. **Single sequins** are sewed on with a bead in the center. Bring the needle up through the fabric. Place a sequin on the needle, then a bead. Slip them down on to the fabric. Stitch back through the center of the sequin.

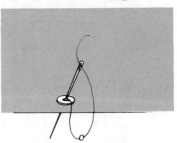

3. **Sequins used in an outline design:** Bring the needle to the right side of the fabric and pick up a sequin. Hold the sequin flat and take a stitch over the edge. Bring the needle to the right side, one half the width of the sequin ahead. As you continue sewing, the edge of each sequin will be overlapped by the next.

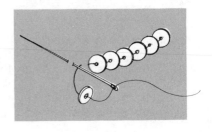

4. When **pressing** a beaded or sequined garment do not place a hot iron directly on the beadwork — it can cause scratching and melting. Avoid pressing at all if possible. If you do, the beadwork should be placed face down on a plush towel and pressed lightly from the wrong side.

Covered Buttons

Before covering the metal button, fuse Stacy's Easyknit interfacing to the fabric. Use this technique for satins, peau de soie and other fabrics that might ravel or "show-through" the shiny metal. For sheers, use a double layer of fabric. Buttons to cover that are sold with a rubber "covering tool" work best. It's much easier to control the fabric because the tool secures it in place around the button.

Buttons That Don't Button

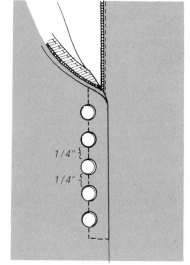

Here's a sneaky way to add button "back interest" to your gown without having to make buttonholes or loops.

Insert a zipper down the center back seam, using a lapped application. Then sew covered buttons down the stitching line about ¼" apart.

Super-Fast Button-Loop Closures

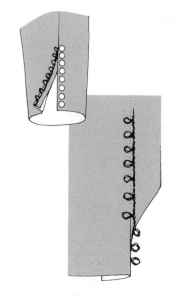

Hooray for readymade elastic button loops! Available in white, these loops take the drudgery out of making this style closure . . . but look just as professional. Since they are covered by the buttons, we don't bother dyeing them to match ivory gowns.

Extend the opening seam allowance to 1" when cutting. Simply sew the elastic edge ⅛" inside the seam allowance. Be careful not to stretch the loop edge while stitching. Sew covered buttons ½" apart on the other side of the seam.

NOTE: If the fit of your gown is too tight, these buttonhole loops will S-T-R-E-T-C-H out exposing you or your undergarments.

Easy-to-Turn Spaghetti Straps and Belts

This technique for turning bias strips is "self-filling" — the seam allowance gives the tube soft body. For most bridal wear, corded tubings are too stiff and tailored looking.

1. Cut bias strips 4½ times the finished width. For sheers, cut the strips 5-6 times the finished width.

2. Trim one end of the bias strip to a point.

3. Securely stitch a string to the pointed end of the strip (the string should be a few inches longer than the strip).

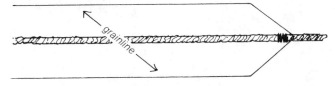

4. Fold the bias strip in half, right sides together, positioning the string down the fold so that at least 1" extends beyond the strip end.

5. Start stitching a little bit wider than the desired finished width, then taper back to the finished width as shown. Do not catch the string in the stitching. The wider stitching will allow the strip to be more easily turned.

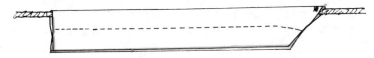

Stretch the seam very slightly as you sew to keep the stitches from popping.

6. Carefully pull the string and turn the tube to the right side.

Bustle Yourself a Danceable Train

One of Karen's friends shared this neat idea for shortening an extended train on an all-over lace gown for reception dancing. This bustle idea can be used on raised, sloping or natural waistlines.

Simply sew hooks and eyes under lace appliques. Eyes are sewn at the waistline 4" from either side of the center back just above the waistline seam. Hooks are sewn upside-down 6" from either side of the center back skirt seam 14-20" down from the waist (the longer the train, the more distance between the hooks and eyes).

After the ceremony, when you're ready to dance, have someone lift and hook the train. Adjust the bustle and cut a rug!

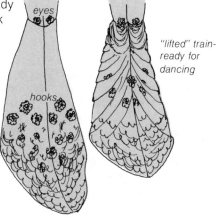

"lifted" train-
ready for
dancing

Another "Lifting" Technique for Trains — Wrist Loops

If your train is cumbersome for moving about or dancing, but not adaptable to the "bustled" effect, try wrist loops. Your hand slips through these loops, lifting the train.

1. Cut a piece of ½" wide satin ribbon 14" long. Fold the ribbon in half lengthwise.

Note: Pin the wrist loop in place before stitching. Try a "test run". Some gowns, when carried in this manner can be too revealing.

2. Machine stitch the doubled ribbon to the train center back seam allowances close to the hem edge.

Lingerie Straps

To prevent bra and slip straps from creeping out during the ceremony or reception, sew in lingerie straps.

Cut a 1½" length of ½" wide satin ribbon, the color of your gown. Handstitch down about ½" as shown, at the armhole edge. Sew a snap to the end of the ribbon and to the shoulder seam allowance.

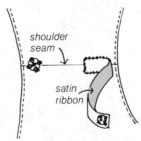

shoulder seam

satin ribbon

Take the Weight Off Your Gown

Many gowns are made of yards and yards of fabric — the weight of the fabric or heavy beading can put a potentially damaging strain on the shoulder seams when hanging. "Hanging" loops can solve this problem:

1. Measure ½" wide seam tape or ribbon twice the length of the bodice front from the waist to the shoulder plus 1" for seam allowances. Cut two.

2. Fold the tape or ribbon in half lengthwise. Sew to both the side waistline seam allowances.

3. Slip the loops over a padded hanger. During wear the loops will hang under the skirt.

XIV.
Headpieces/Veils

Easy to Make, Expensive to Buy

The headpiece "finishes" the traditional bridal look; it draws attention to your face, flattering any size or shape bride. Even if you don't sew anything else for your wedding, you should consider making the headpiece and veil. Headpieces require minimal time and sewing skills, yet the savings in relation to ready-mades are amazing!

A chapel-length veil and headpiece you make for $12.00 can cost you $80.00 ready-made in a bridal shop (see page 7). We also priced a derby hat covered with lace, illusion and Qiana jersey that retailed from $90.00. In a fabric store the basic derby hat cost $9.50. Adding two yards of illusion fabric and lace scraps from a gown, we could make the same hat for a total cost of $14.00 — a savings of $76.00. And it only took two hours to make!

Style Selection

The range of headpiece styles is vast and constantly changing. In one catalogue alone there were 150 styles shown! Although some bridal consultants try to tell you a certain headpiece is definitely "in fashion" that season, choose a style and veil length that's "you" — flattering and compatible with your wedding type and gown. Try on readymade headpieces, veils and hats to help you decide on a style.

You may want just a decorated frame, hat or veil — or a combination of all three. Some brides decide to wear no headpiece at all, but rather a flower, ribbon or special hairdo. And as we've said before, study bride's magazines . . . they're chock full of veil and headpiece style ideas.

Frames

The headpiece begins as an inexpensive frame made of buckram or wire in a variety of styles. Use your left-over lace and fabric scraps, appliqués and beads to glue or stitch to the frame. Veils may or may not be attached. Try on the frame to find one that best suits your face structure and gown style. Remember that a covered frame can be a headpiece in itself . . . veiling is not a must.

Types of Frames

NOTE: Fabric stores usually carry buckram or fabric-covered frames. Craft stores and catalogues carry more "uncovered" wire frames. You'll find fabric covered or buckram frames are easier to recover than wire frames. Use wire frames for "see-through" lace and flower headpieces.

These frames all fit the Traceable Bride (see page 31).

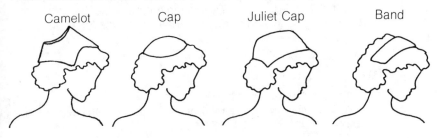

Camelot   Cap   Juliet Cap   Band

Wreath
(often covered with flowers,
either real or artificial)

Beautiful fabric-covered, lace-trimmed
headpieces are also available in fabric
stores if time is too short to make
your own.

Covering the Frame the Glue Way

1. Decide on the style of frame and veil style/length.

2. Purchase the frame and fabric/appliqués, beads, etc. for covering (you will probably be able to use fabric scraps).

3. To cut the fabric to size, roll the frame onto the bias line of the fabric. With tailors chalk, trace around the frame, allowing a ½" seam allowance.

4. Cut out the fabric along the marked lines. Press the fabric to remove any wrinkles.

5. On the underside of the frame, dot the edge with glue. Allow the glue to dry for a minute or so.

6. Starting at the center of the frame, attach the wrong side of the fabric seam allowance to the glue. Work from side to side, stretching the fabric across the frame — it should be taut, with no wrinkles.

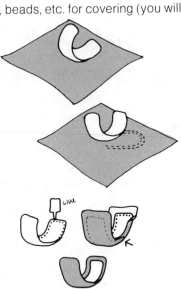

7. Clip off any excess fabric and add extra glue where necessary.

8. Your frame is covered. Now you can add lace, trim or beads. Simply position them (use tape to position lace as you're designing) and glue! Scissor-style tweezers make the job of applying pearls and beads a whole lot easier (see page 105).

The Allure of Hats

The glamorous derby, a charming picture hat . . . the wedding hat is the newest fashion statement. Marrying out-of-doors? A picture hat keeps the sun off your freckles! These hats all fit the Traceable Bride (see page 31).

Types of Hats

Picture   Derby   Turban

Pillbox   Toque   Wreath

NOTE: Small hats look best with facial veiling only. Derby and picture hats can have a facial veil and/or veil floating off the back. Russian net and point d' esprit net coordinate well with hats in an updated look.

Trimming a Hat

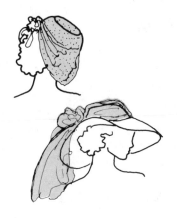

- When using fabric to trim a hat, cut it on the bias for softness. Don't worry about netting. It has no grainline.

- Softly drape with a sheer fabric or net and tack with long basting stitches to secure. Lace, flowers or ribbon can cover the joining seam.

- For a picture hat, wrap a length of soft fabric or fine net (illusion or tulle) around the crown. Crush into soft folds and hand-baste to the crown (the ends can extend from these folds to form a veil effect).

- Wrap a narrow folded length (30" × 108") of illusion around the brim. Tie in a bow, or gently "pouf" the netting and secure to the hat, leaving streamers down the back.

- Flowers and ribbon streamers are a very simple way to adorn hats.

- Attach veils to hats at the back, coming from under or from the top (see page 118). Try different placements of the veil on the hat until you find the look that is most flattering.

The Veil

The custom of a bride wearing a veil started during the days when strangers were "matched" for marriage. The bride was "delivered" to the ceremony, and the groom was not allowed to "unveil" his bride until they were man and wife.

Since that time veils have evolved into wedding fashion, very much a part of the classic bridal look. Like gowns, there are literally hundreds of different veil styles. Try some on in ready-to-wear shops before deciding on the style to make.

You'll notice that the pattern companies have very few veil patterns. As you might imagine, a very large and long veil would require an awful lot of tissue paper! What we know is that for most veil styles you don't need a pattern, simply dimensions and general shape guidelines. If you are uncertain how long to make your veil, cut it long, try it on and keep shortening until it's just the right length.

NOTE: Some of the most intricate and detailed mantillas look best when worn with very plain gowns. In turn, some of the frilliest, most romantic gowns look best when worn with plain headpieces. Your gown and headpiece should complement, not fight each other.

Veil Fabrics

The most commonly used veil fabrics are illusion and tulle. Illusion is softest, most drapeable and most versatile because of its width (up to 144" wide).

Name		Characteristics	Uses
Illusion 　Nylon 　and 　Silk (72", 108" 144" wide)		• Fine delicate mesh • Nylon crisper 　than silk type • Available in white 　and candlelight • Silk is expensive	• Most veils • Bindings for laces • Background for lace 　appliques • Used for full 　gathered veils because 　no piecing is required
Tulle (54" wide)		• Thicker mesh 　than illusion • Available in 　many colors	• Rice bags • Backing and bindings 　for laces • Attendants' headpieces
Maline (27" wide)		• Medium size mesh • Available in many 　colors	• Draped over hats • Facial veils
Net (72" wide)		• Coarse and crisp 　mesh • Available in many 　colors • Inexpensive	• Almond bags • Underskirt ruffles for 　slips (see Chapter 　XII)
Point d' esprit (72" wide)		• Net or tulle 　with dot design • Available in 　selected colors	• Dramatic veils • Gown bodice or fabric • Backing for lace
English Net (72" wide)		• Fine cotton net • Has a garden/ 　country look • Soft texture	• Gown fabric • Hat adornment • Mantilla
French Net (9" wide)		• Wide mesh • Limited color 　selections	• Draped over hats • Facial veils

Length

Although there are many veil styles, there are five basic lengths:

Facial/Madonna/Blusher
often combined with others
for semi-formal and formal
weddings

Ballerina/Waltz/Elbow
(elbow length)
for short and/or
informal gowns

Fingertip length
for semi-formal
and formal
weddings

Chapel length
(to the floor)
for semi-formal and
formal weddings

Cathedral length
(1 ft. or more on the floor)
for formal weddings

Veil Styles

NOTE: All veil lengths given are average; compare to your height.

Mantilla (pronounced MAN TEE YA) A true mantilla is made completely of lace and should be worn with a classic, clean-line gown. Now, however, mantillas, for the most part, are made with a wide lace edging. A mantilla is not usually worn with a frame. When it is, the frame is worn under the mantilla for height (camelot and juliet styles are common).

Pattern

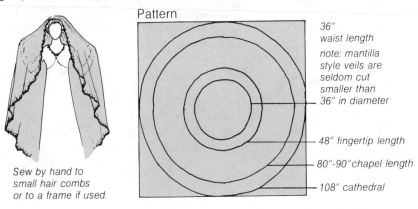

*Sew by hand to
small hair combs
or to a frame if used.*

*36"
waist length
note: mantilla
style veils are
seldom cut
smaller than
36" in diameter*

48" fingertip length

80"-90" chapel length

108" cathedral

"Pouf" Veil This is a veil that is very "pouffy" through the crown. Many short brides like this style because it adds height. Cut short, this style can be a "blusher" or facial veil.

Gather along top edge and sew by hand to the frame or, if plain, to small hair combs.

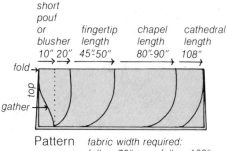

short pouf or blusher 10" 20"	fingertip length 45" 50"	chapel length 80"-90"	cathedral length 108"

fold→
top
gather→

Pattern   fabric width required:
full — 72"; very full — 108"
for blusher — 40"-54"

Basic Drape Veil By far the most popular of all the veils, this type can be attached to any frame or hat. It is less gathered through the crown than the pouf veil.

The straight top edge creates less "pouf" than a curved top edge.

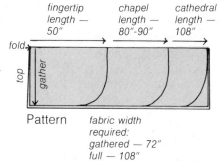

fingertip length — 50"	chapel length — 80"-90"	cathedral length — 108"

fold→
top
gather

Pattern   fabric width required:
gathered — 72"
full — 108"
very full — 144"

NOTE: An easy way to gather the edge and attach the veil. For any of the gathered styles, use this technique for gathering up the edge. Set your machine on a long wide zig-zag. Stitch over white polyester buttonhole twist, enclosing but not catching the heavier thread. Secure one end of the buttonhole twist. Draw up the edge by pulling the buttonhole twist. Leave the end of the heavy thread long for sewing to the frame, comb, hat, etc.

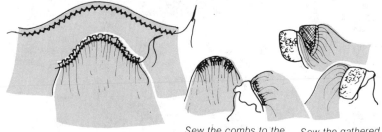

Sew the combs to the gathered edge with long whipstitch.

Sew the gathered veil to a frame under the back edge.

Updated Veil For those of you who prefer a veil with less "pouf", this is a good style. The back is slightly longer than the sides. As with all veil styles, it can be cut any length.

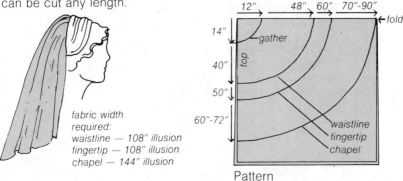

fabric width required:
waistline — 108" illusion
fingertip — 108" illusion
chapel — 144" illusion

Pattern

Double-Layer Veil This veil has fewer gathers, so it drapes or hangs down, rather than lending height. This style can be "frameless". Because it has fewer bulky gathers, it can be easily sewn to hair combs.

Try draping two layers of veiling together (we suggest illusion for this style) to decide if you like this look — it will appear "whiter" and heavier than a single layer veil.

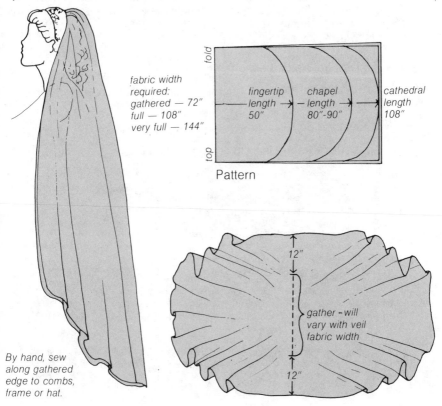

fabric width required:
gathered — 72"
full — 108"
very full — 144"

Pattern

By hand, sew along gathered edge to combs, frame or hat.

Veil Edgings

Leave the edge plain since veil fabrics do not ravel. Be sure to cut the edge evenly. An untrimmed veil will be "pouffier" because it doesn't have a trim on the edge weighting it down.

Edge tracing: Fold under ⅜" and stitch around the edge of the veil with a narrow zig-zag. Trim excess hem close to stitching with embroidery scissors. The fine white line defines the outside edge of the veil without adding much weight. Needless to say, this edge treatment is economical too!

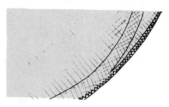

Lace trim: Lovely around the outside edge of a veil and easy to apply. Our only word of warning is "your veil shouldn't over-power your gown" . . . sometimes the addition of yards and yards of lace around the outside edge of a veil can make it too busy. Pin the lace on at least half of the veil edge. Then put on the veil and your gown. Stand in front of a mirror — is this the look you want? If it is, apply the lace as follows:

1. Apply the lace before gathering the top edge of the veil.

2. Lap the wrong side of the lace over the right side of the veil edge. (Use a lace that is finished on both edges.)

3. Set your machine on 8 stitches per inch.

4. Topstitch the lace to the veil. Don't stretch the edge.

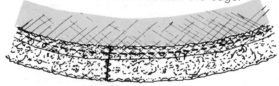

NOTE: If piecing of the lace is necessary, "butt" the edges and zig-zag together rather than standard seaming. The result will be a flatter, less conspicuous seam that's hidden in the lace pattern.

NOTE: Individual lace motifs can be scattered throughout the veil. Apply with glue.

XV.
Other Members
of the Bridal Party

Mothers of the Bride and Groom

For most mothers the wedding day is exciting, nerve-racking, tearful and wonderfully fun. Their role is to assist the couple in last minute details and serve as greeters at the reception.

They want to look and feel their very best at the ceremony. Choosing the right color and style gown that harmonizes with the entire "wedding look" is therefore an important decision. Tradition states that the bride's mother chooses her dress first, then contacts the groom's mother to fill her in on the choice. Their dress colors should not clash although they need not be the same style. Lengths, however, should be the same.

Styles

- Mothers needn't be dowdy! Don't be afraid of an "upbeat" look.

- Follow our Figure Flattery Recommendations . . . even sketch the gown using the "Traceable Bride" silhouette (see page 31).

- Evening wear designs are excellent design sources.

- Back interest is not important on mothers' gowns.

- Consider outfits — blouse and skirt, a jacketed dress, a dressy suit.

- Avoid revealing necklines.

Fabrics

- Cool weather — crepe, knits (not too clingy), silks, velvet, brocades.

- Warm weather — sheers, soft knits, linen, lightweight crepe, cottons.

Color

- Blue and apricot are the most popular. Darker shades aren't taboo.

- Keep the flower colors and attendants' gowns in mind

- Dresses should blend with, but not match the bridesmaids'.

- Solid colors should be worn if the bridesmaids' dresses are a print.

Accessories

- Comfortable shoes that match or blend with your outfit.

- Gloves are optional.

- Small clutches are handy and less cumbersome than a purse.

- Flowers for mothers are usually a corsage worn on the dress or in the hair.

- Keep jewelry simple and elegant (accent the face, not the lower body).

- Hats are optional. If worn, they should be small and becoming from all angles (don't hide under a hat!).

- Wraps can be worn to the wedding but should be taken off during the ceremony.

NOTE: Grandmothers can follow these style guidelines too.

The Scene Stealers . . . Children

Styles

- Pick a basic style and add ribbon, ruffles, lace, etc.

- A detachable pinafore or fancy vest can make the outfits more convertible to later use.

- For little girls, check out the night-gown styles . . . in the right fabric they can look dressed up and so feminine.

- Use lace from the bridal gown for the flower girl's dress or the ring-bearer's pillow.

- Make the ringbearer's shirt and buy the rest of the outfit. The shirt can coordinate with the flower girl's dress.

- If you do make the ringbearer's jacket, choose an easy cardigan style or vest.

- Both girls and boys can be minia-ture versions of the bridesmaids and ushers.

Accessories

- For the flower girl, a small bouquet or basket of flowers.

- For the ringbearer, the ring pillow.

- Shoes and socks that match or blend.

- A small headpiece and gloves for the flower girl are optional.

Color

- Can match or blend with the wedding party.

- Scale down the size of the print.

- Let the ruffle or trim highlight the primary wedding color.

- Flower girls can be "all-white" like the bride, with a bouquet color accent.

Accessory Ideas

Pattern companies now offer patterns for all the bridal accessories — look for them in the bridal or crafts catalogue sections.

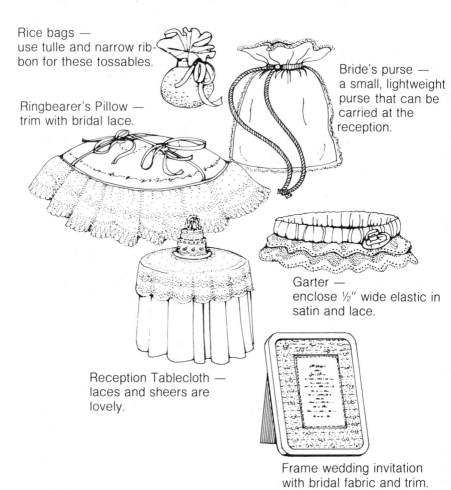

Rice bags —
use tulle and narrow ribbon for these tossables.

Ringbearer's Pillow —
trim with bridal lace.

Bride's purse —
a small, lightweight purse that can be carried at the reception.

Garter —
enclose ½" wide elastic in satin and lace.

Reception Tablecloth —
laces and sheers are lovely.

Frame wedding invitation with bridal fabric and trim.